Why Does Everybody Hate Me?

Why Does Everybody Hate Me?

KAREN DOCKREY

ZondervanPublishingHouse
Grand Rapids, Michigan

A Division of HarperCollinsPublishers

Why Does Everybody Hate Me?
Copyright © 1991 by Karen Dockrey

Published by Zondervan Publishing House
1415 Lake Drive, S.E., Grand Rapids, Michigan 49506

Library of Congress Cataloging-in-Publication Data

Dockrey, Karen, 1955–
    Why does everybody hate me?/by Karen Dockrey
      p. cm.
    Summary: Discusses how to combat feelings of loneliness and low
self-esteem by choosing to grow close to God and to other people.
    ISBN 0–310–54111–5
      1. Loneliness in adolescence—Miscellanea—Juvenile litera-
ture. 2. Self-respect in adolescence—Miscellanea—Juvenile
literature. 3. Interpersonal relations in adolescence—Miscellanea—Juvenile literature. 4 Teenagers—Religious life—Miscellanea—Juvenile literature. [1. Loneliness. 2. Self-respect.
3. Interpersonal relations.   4. Christian life.]   I. Title.
BF724.3.L64D63   1991   248.8'3—dc20
                                                          CIP
                                                           AC
Edited by Lori Walburg and Rose Pruiksma
Designed by The Church Art Works ™
Cover design by Terry Dugan Design
Inside illustrations by Corbin Hillam

Printed in the United States of America

91 92 93 94 95 96 / ML / 10 9 8 7 6 5 4 3 2 1

Dedicated to
Emily and Sarah
and to
the youth of Bluegrass Baptist Church
with a prayer that you'll believe the quality
God has created in each of you

About the YouthSource™ Publishing Group

YouthSource™ books, tapes, videos, and other resources pool the expertise of three of the finest youth-ministry resource providers in the world:

Campus Life Books—publishers of the award-winning *Campus Life* magazine, for nearly fifty years helping high schoolers live Christian lives.

Youth Specialties—serving ministers to middle school, junior high, and high school for over twenty years through books, magazines, and training events such as the National Youth Workers Convention.

Zondervan Publishing House—one of the oldest, largest, and most respected evangelical Christian publishers in the world.

Campus Life	**Youth Specialties**	**Zondervan**
465 Gundersen Dr.	1224 Greenfield Dr.	1415 Lake Dr., S.E.
Carol Stream, IL 60188	El Cajon, CA 92021	Grand Rapids, MI 49506
708/260-6200	619/440-2333	616/698-6900

TABLE OF
CONTENTS

Introduction

Does it sometimes seem like everybody hates you? Do your parents, friends, dates, and teachers all seem out to get you? Do you even hate yourself?

You don't have to just sit and take it. You can fight those negative feelings by choosing to grow close to God and to other people. The fight won't be easy. And you won't win right away. But you *will* win.

Using real-life examples, this book will help you win your battle against hurt feelings and loneliness. You'll learn that the cure for loneliness takes two steps. First, you need to begin and grow a relationship with God. In the end, only God can relieve your loneliness. Even having dozens of friends won't help you fill that deep-down empty feeling that only God can fill.

Second, once you have God, look for friends and family members who care for you and let you care for them. Matthew 6:33 says, "Seek first his kingdom and his righteousness, and all these things will be given to you as well." If you look for God first, he will show you the people who can help ease your loneliness.

You can make your own happiness. Happiness is not what happens to you—it's what you *do* with what happens to you. Using God as your anchor, you can feel loved even when it seems like the whole world is against you—and even when it feels like everybody hates you.

I'm the Only One Home on Weekend Nights

When you're all alone, you may feel like no one anywhere wants anything to do with you. But being lonely doesn't mean you're worthless any more than feeling sick means you'll never be well again. When you're sick, you go to the doctor, who diagnoses what is wrong and prescribes a treatment. In the same way, when you're lonely, you can diagnose and treat those lonely feelings. Read on to find out how.

■

Overcoming Loneliness

I'm fine as long as I stay busy, but as soon as I'm alone and quiet, I feel desperately lonely. Activity hides my pain. When I'm alone, I worry that no one who really knew me could love me.

Loneliness is a pain—literally. It hurts. And when you hurt, you'll do almost anything to get rid of the pain. Some people drown their hurt in alcohol. Other people cling to their boyfriend or girlfriend. Other people, like you, bury themselves in their work.

But all those things are just distractions. You can't be drunk all the time (although some people try!); you can't be with your boyfriend or girlfriend all the time (eventually you have to go home or hang up the phone); and, as you've discovered, you can't stay busy all the time. So where do you turn when your distractions don't distract you anymore?

I have found that mastering loneliness begins with God. When you're lonely, you yearn for someone who really understands what you think and feel, and who loves you even after he knows you. God is this someone. Family, friends, and dates can understand a lot about you, but only God can understand you fully. In fact, he understands even what you don't understand about yourself. Thank him for this understanding and ask him to share it with you.

Remember, though, that God isn't enough. He created us to

need other people. God said of Adam, "It is not good for the man to be alone." And that's when he made Eve. First God built his relationship with Adam. Then he showed Adam how to love Eve.

Building a relationship with God and learning to love people work hand in hand. As the following diagram shows, your relationships intersect, with *you* in the middle. The side arrows represent your relationships with family, friends, teachers, and bosses. The up arrow represents you relating to God. The down arrow represents God relating to you. As you keep the up arrow straight, you'll keep your human relationships healthy and happy.

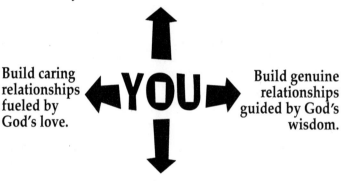

**Turn to God to find the security
you need to reach out to others.**

**Build caring
relationships
fueled by
God's love.**

YOU

**Build genuine
relationships
guided by God's
wisdom.**

**Let God teach you
how to relate to others.**

Building relationships with God and others is a big order; it takes time, commitment, and know-how. This book will give you some of the know-how. You add the time and commitment. In the following chapters I'll talk about what to do in specific situations. As you work through your challenges, lean on God for guidance, power, and security. And thank him as you see your relationships grow.

■

Loneliness:
Causes and Cures

Everybody is out with friends but me. I'm sitting at home feeling sorry for myself. I know self-pity isn't the answer, but I don't know what else to do. How can I get people to like me?

When you're lonely, just as when you're sick, you need to diagnose and treat yourself. The medicine for fixing loneliness depends on the reason you're lonely. Let these sample cases help you diagnose and heal your loneliness:

CAUSE

You're by yourself and want to be with somebody.

You had a fight with someone you care about, and you both need time to cool off before you talk further.

You fear you are boring company.

Everyone is at an event but you. Or your best friend is out of town.

CURE

Call a friend or spend time with a family member.

Take time to cool off, writing or doodling your feelings. Then talk out that disagreement.

Go somewhere with a group so the burden of "being fun" doesn't weigh so heavily upon your shoulders.

Let yourself grieve. Have a good cry, and then find something else to do.

You don't enjoy your own company.	Remind yourself that God made you good and lovable. Pray for the courage to make this apparent to yourself and others. Read chapter 9 of this book.
Someone you like went out with someone besides you. Or a friend has a date and you don't.	Let yourself be sad and disappointed for a little while, and then invite another friend over and do something fun.
You've just moved to a new community or school and don't know anyone yet.	Remind yourself that it takes time to feel at home in a new place. Decide to get to know at least one person better before the next Friday night rolls around.
You couldn't find anything to do.	Check out what's going on at church or enroll in a class to learn what you've always wanted to learn.
You keep getting mad at friends.	Find ways to talk about problems instead of letting them separate you (see chapter 2).
You decided to stay home to take a break from the hectic pace but now find yourself lonely.	Remind yourself why you're there and do what you had in mind. See suggestions later in this chapter.
You're having trouble overcoming shyness.	Force yourself to go somewhere with a group or to call a friend you like.
You're waiting for someone to make the first move.	That someone is probably waiting for you. Even the most confident-looking people are basically shy and wonder if you'll be offended if they call. Make the first move.

You didn't think about going anywhere until this afternoon and now everyone is busy.	Plan ahead for next weekend. For now, do something interesting by yourself or with a family member.
Whatever is going on does not interest you.	Find something else to do with someone else who skipped the activity.
Your friends are out without you by accident.	Discover the reason. Maybe your phone was busy when they tried to call. Maybe it was a spontaneous get-together after the game you couldn't go to. Maybe you were supposed to go out of town. Wait until next time.
Your friends didn't call on purpose.	Discover and remedy the reasons. Maybe they're fair-weather friends. Maybe you've been treating them badly, driving them away with cutdowns and sarcasm. Perhaps you always demand that they do things your way. Maybe you do all the talking and never listen. Perhaps you act so self-assured they assume you don't want them around. Make changes. Notice your friends' needs. Replace cuts with compliments. Alternate your plans with your friends' plans. Listen as well as talk. Be real rather than protecting a perfect image. You can't change what has already happened, but you can apologize, you can change the present, and you can refuse to let the past doom the future.

Why Does Everybody Hate Me?

Alone Times

Sometimes I'm home alone because I don't want to be with people. At times like that I don't have the energy to be around anyone. Is that OK?

During times of sadness, frustration, fatigue, or chaos it's natural to want to be alone. In fact, being alone and sorting through feelings and thoughts with God is important for renewal and healing. Times you may need to be alone include:

1. *After a major spiritual event such as a church retreat or mission trip.* You feel emotionally and spiritually exhausted. You need to be alone to rest, sleep, and reflect. In 1 Kings 18–19 we read that Elijah, after a big spiritual victory, felt discouraged and depressed. God prescribed rest, food, and later a friend named Elisha to help.

2. *Following an overnight band trip, major ball tournament, or other grueling physical activity.* You need rest to recover.

3. *When someone you love has died.* Use your time alone to sort out your thoughts and cry freely. Ecclesiastes 3:4 reminds us to take time to mourn. Because you also need care from friends and family, balance alone time with people time.

4. *When you or someone you love is very ill.* Take some time alone to pray, to grieve, to recover.

5. *When you need time to think.* When you need to make a major decision or when you simply need to take a closer look at your life, you need to be alone to think.

Alone time becomes detrimental when it is a steady diet. Times you need to push yourself to be with others include:

- When you've moved to a new home and don't know anyone yet.

- When you've been alone for a good reason but have stayed alone too long. For example, you might need a week to be alone after a breakup, but then you need to get out and start going places again.

- When you're at a new school.

- When you're shy and find it easier to be by yourself.

Some people get worn out when they're around other people all the time and need to be by themselves to recover. They are called introverts. Other people like to be around other people almost all the time, and they panic when they're by themselves. They are called extroverts. Neither one nor the other kind of person is better. Both introverts and extroverts need to balance alone time with people time to be happy. Find the balance that works for you.

■

Making the Most of Alone Times

There are times I really don't want to go out or am not interested in what everyone else is doing. I don't have trouble deciding to stay home, but once I find myself there, I'm miserable. Why does this happen? What should I do?

First, compliment yourself for choosing what to do with your evening. Everyone needs alone time to recharge, to create, to dream, to ponder, to work on interests, to think things through, to get lost in a book, to plan, to just be. As you invite God to do all these things with you, the benefits of alone time multiply.

Second, recognize that physical aloneness, even for a good reason, can make you feel lonely. You may want company, not demanding company, but someone near you. Why is your yearning for people strong, even when you want to be alone? Because, as I mentioned earlier, human beings are made to be around other people. When God made Eve as a companion for Adam, God did so because he knew that it was not good for people to be alone (Genesis 2:18).

You need family and friends for companionship. Companionship can mean anything from just being with someone to getting into a deep conversation. Perhaps all you need is the presence of your parent in the next room to give you the companionship you need. Or you may want your parent to listen to you as you dream, think, and plan.

What kind of loneliness are you experiencing? Do you want the comfort of someone nearby? Someone to listen to you? Someone to work with you on your project? Someone in the same room without talking? Do you want God's presence? Seek the kind of companionship you need. If no one is around or everyone is busy, schedule something for later. Even when no family member is available, God is. He can't take the place of a human, but he can definitely ease your loneliness.

Your lonely feelings may mean you need something meaningful to do. Choose something you enjoy and dive in. If you aren't sure what that is, try several things to help you discover what you like. Here are some things other teens have done during alone times:

- "I think of all the people and circumstances I'm angry about as I work out on my exercise equipment. By the time I finish exercising, I've worked out my anger."

- "I get lost in a book. A good book can make me feel good about who I am and the choices I make."

- "I relax with whatever I feel like doing at the moment. Sometimes it's going through my comic book collection or sorting my coins. Doing what I want to do at the pace I want to do it helps me get ready for the next challenge."

- "I write in my journal. Putting my thoughts down helps me understand myself."

- "I write letters. Writing letters means I'll get letters back, which means I'll feel less lonely at mail time."

- "I watch TV or listen to tapes. When I choose the right shows and songs, I feel better."

What interest, project, hobby, or relaxing activity makes your alone time meaningful? What can you dream about, plan, or ponder? What spiritual question do you want to understand better? Take time to let your mind and body cruise or explore. It makes the hectic pace of your life more livable.

The Point: Physical aloneness can create loneliness. But alone time doesn't have to be lonely time. It can become exhilarating when you turn it into an opportunity for creating, relaxing, dreaming, or exploring. It can also be a chance to make changes that will help you in your next together time with family or friends.

 # Think It Through

1. What's the difference between being alone and being lonely? When do you like being alone? When do you hate it?

2. Why is God the only one who can ultimately relieve your loneliness? What's the danger of depending on a single person for relief from loneliness?

3. How does closeness with God enhance friendships? How do quality friendships enhance your relationship with God?

4. What was the cause of your last loneliness? What did you do to solve it? What else might have helped even more?

5. When do you need to be alone? When do you need to push yourself to be with people?

6. What makes it easy for you to believe and live the truths in Matthew 6:33 and Psalm 139? What makes it hard?

Even When I Go Places, I Still Feel Lonely

Did you ever feel lonely even when you were surrounded by your friends? It's a confusing loneliness. When no one is around, you understand the reason for your loneliness. But when you're surrounded by perfectly happy-looking people and you feel miserable, you begin to wonder what's wrong with you. "Do they like me?" "Why won't anyone talk to me?" "What am I doing here?" "I wish I could go home."

There's always a reason for feeling lonely in a crowd. Maybe the crowd has different interests. Maybe you just moved to the area and need time to get to know people. Maybe you don't get along with one person in the crowd and that colors everything else. Maybe you need to work your way out of shyness. Maybe you need to practice people skills. To solve your lonely-in-a-crowd agony, recognize that people skills, like any other skills, take practice. Spend time in groups to learn how to feel at home. And check out the questions below to get more tips about how to feel comfortable in a crowd.

■

Fitting In

Everybody else seems comfortable, but I just don't fit in. What's wrong with me? How can I feel like I belong? Where can I find real friends?

Believe it or not, even people who look comfortable are also having trouble feeling like they fit. We all put on our happy faces when we go out. Knowing that everyone feels uncomfortable and self-conscious at first can make it easier for you to deal with those feelings.

Besides, fitting in and *feeling* like you fit in are two different things. Stephanie was incredibly likable and fun to be around. Although they didn't tell her often, Stephanie's friends loved her smile, her laughter, her ideas. Her friends were devastated and bewildered when Stephanie tried to kill herself. She thought that no one really cared. Stephanie fit in, but she didn't *feel* like she fit in.

So how do you go about making yourself *feel* like you fit in? Listen to adults and friends who tell you your good points. At the same time, build up other people by saying hello, telling them what you like about them, calling to say you missed them when they didn't come, giving compliments, being there, and sending notes.

"But wait a minute," you say, "I'm the one worrying about fitting in! Why are you talking about others?" Because focusing on others will help you feel at home with yourself. Rather than seeing people as ways to ease *your* loneliness, see yourself as a way to ease *their* loneliness. It's not easy, but it works! Invite someone who's sitting alone to sit at your lunch table. Start a conversation with someone who seems to be lonely. As you turn outside yourself, you'll find that you have the loving skills needed to make others happy. That, in turn, will make you happy. And others will like being around you.

Be friendly to everyone, but for closer friends look for people who have similar interests. Go ice skating to get in contact with other figure skaters. Take karate lessons to meet other green belts hoping to be black belts. Compete in math contests to find friends who enhance your logical thinking skills. Get around people who do the things you like to do. The more alike you are, the more you'll feel like you fit, and the better you can encourage and understand each other. The most important similarity is Christian faith. If you're both seeking to follow God, you'll learn friend-making from the best teacher, God himself.

When you are around people who are different from you, find something you have in common. It may be a feeling you share ("I worry about being accepted too."), an attraction you feel ("I love girls with freckles too!"), or a skill you share ("You mean you like geometry too?") We're all more alike than we are different.

Focus on others, find people with similar interests, and look for the common things all people share. These three friend-making skills become easier as you focus on God. Psalm 37:4 encourages you to "delight yourself in the Lord and he will give you the desires of your heart." God wants to help you become comfortable with yourself and others. He wants you to feel joy and peace. As people notice these qualities in you, they'll want to be around you.

Reread Psalm 37:4. Remember: As you delight yourself in God, he'll give you your heart's desires—including true friends and caring dates.

■

Locker-Room Loneliness

This is kind of a weird crowd question, but I get lonely in the locker room because I can't join in the talk. A guy had sex for the first time Friday night. Somebody else did it last weekend, and the guys keep asking when I'm going to do it. How can I say that I plan to remain faithful to the wife I've never met? That sounds totally boring compared to their escapades. I want to obey God's guidelines for building true love, but it seems like I'm the only one. Everyone else goes to bed with their girlfriends. They think I'm crazy to still be a virgin.

This is one of those times you *don't* want to fit in! You're smart to recognize God's guidelines as the only path to happiness. You're also smart to realize that following God isn't easy. It's harder to wait for sex than to give in and have it now. It's harder to *build* love than to *make* love. Choosing the harder path leads to love that lasts a lifetime. You not only want this love; you need it. You shortchange yourself if you do any less.

You may feel like you're swimming upstream. Keep swimming. If enough people begin to swim against the tide, the direction of the flow can turn. As more and more of us commit to living out the Bible's principles, truly loving relationships will grow—a goal worth working toward.

You need a friend to encourage you. Find at least one friend with the same commitment to wait until marriage to have sex. Share your ideas on dating and love. Encourage each other. And keep living your commitment, knowing you've made the right choice.

■

Party Talk

How can I get started talking to people at parties? I know I'm supposed to just be friendly, but it's hard for me. I work up my confidence before I go, but then I freeze up. Will I ever become comfortable talking to people?

I understand how you feel. I too was once very shy with new people. Making friends comes easily for some, but for most of us it is a gradual process full of both apprehension and hope. The positive factor is that God is intensely interested in the friends we make. Because he created love, he knows how to help you love people and help others love you.

The best way to begin a conversation is to smile, say hello, and ask a question. "How was your day?" "Who's your favorite in the student council election?" "How do you think the game will go?" "How did you do on the pop quiz?" When possible, ask paragraph questions—questions that need more than a "yes" or "no" answer, and that encourage discussion.

Some people like to pay a genuine compliment before asking questions: "I'm glad you came" or "You look really good tonight." Smiles, compliments, and interest questions are simple but powerful friendship builders because they put people at ease and show we care.

Smiling, paying compliments, and asking questions sounds easy, but as you well know, they can be agonizingly hard. Rather than expect instant results, take it in steps. At the next party, talk to one person you haven't talked with before. Review what went well and congratulate yourself. During the next party talk to two people, four people the next, and so on. Build your courage gradually. One boy said, "I was so shy at first that it took me a week to get the courage to talk to one person. As my confidence built and as people didn't turn away when I talked to them, I became able to smile at everyone I met." When you blow it, review and learn from your mistake.

As you attempt to make conversation, remember talking is a two-way process. When someone doesn't talk much in return, don't automatically blame yourself. Some people, especially people who like you, may also be shy about talking. Talk briefly and then try again another time.

It may help to "cruise" the party first—saying hello and talking with several people. Notice people who smile in response to your smiles, who like answering your questions, who seem to want to talk to you. Then return to those you were most comfortable with and who seemed most interested in you. Build deeper friendships with those who respond positively to you.

As you talk to people, use their names. Jot names down if you can't remember them. The word people most like to hear is their own name.

I cannot overemphasize the value of focusing on others' comfort. Think about things you want friends to say to you, and say those things (be genuine—people can tell if you're just playing up to them). Most people are as shy as you or more so. Your willingness to speak first can put them at ease and open the door to comfortable conversation. Party by party and day by day, reach out to people. As you focus on others, you will forget your own discomfort. You will discover that people really do like talking to you.

■

Practicing Conversation

I'm kind of shy and have trouble saying what I want to say, so I practice conversations in my head. Am I crazy? If I think through things ahead of time I have less chance of looking dumb. My problem is that the way I practice the conversation in my head is not always the way it comes out.

No, you're not crazy. In fact, I think you're brilliant. If more of us would think through our words before we say them, we'd hurt each other less often and help each other more. Practicing helps you say what you mean to say.

The glitch in your plan, as you have discovered, is real life never goes exactly as we imagine it. To overcome this, imagine as many possibilities as you can and then learn to be flexible. For example, when asking a friend to work with you on a project after school, imagine that he says yes, says no, or hedges and says nothing. Each response could have several reasons:

1. *Yes.* He might say yes because he trusts you, because you asked, because he's complimented by your invitation, because he wants to work with you.

2. *No.* He might say no because he has already finished the project, because he is not far enough along to work with someone else, because he doesn't want to work with you, or because he works better alone.

3. *Hedge.* He might hedge because he knows he has something else to do, because he's already agreed to work with another partner and doesn't want to hurt your feelings, or because he was daydreaming and can't remember what the school project is.

When your friend says yes, thank God that things went as you hoped and say, "Good! I'll look forward to it."

When your friend hedges or says no, use flexibility and questions. Try questions like:

- "Would another time be better?"

- "Is there some reason you can't?"

- "Do you already have a partner?"

- "If you've started, can you give me tips?"

- "Would you rather do something else together?"

Just as practicing conversations in your head makes you feel safer talking to people, practicing conversations in real life grows real-life closeness.

■

Brunt of the Jokes

I have trouble in crowds because I'm the brunt of the jokes. Everyone calls me an airhead and laughs when I say something stupid. I'll admit I am a little spacey sometimes, but I do have a brain. I laugh along when they tease me, but inside it hurts. What did I do to deserve this?

You did nothing to deserve it. You may have been distracted the last time someone talked to you, but that's no reason for continual teasing. These actions may help:

1. *Quit laughing.* People have no way of knowing what's going on inside you except by your behavior. If you laugh, they assume you enjoy the joke. Some may tease you just to hear you laugh. When you stop laughing, your teasers may realize their words hurt. If someone asks why you aren't laughing, gently but seriously say, "I've been laughing because I didn't know what else to do. I decided to stop because it really does hurt when you say those things." Your friends may get embarrassed, defensive, feel sorry, or tease you again. Try to understand the reasons for their behavior just like you want them to understand you.

2. *Talk privately to your friends.* One at a time, ask your friends to stop teasing you about your thinking ability. Explain that it makes you feel stupid, which makes you act stupid, which embarrasses you. Begin with the friend you know best. People who understand tend to do what you need.

3. *Pray for endurance.* Sometimes no matter what you say or

do, people tease anyway. Take it good-naturedly, but don't play along. Many people really mean to show love through teasing. Others follow the cut-down pattern they hear continuously. Our society makes an art out of sarcasm—but this art form enriches no one.

4. *Use words sensitively.* Your pain makes you aware of the power of words. Use your words to build up, not tear down. Ephesians 4:29 says, "Do not let any unwholesome talk come out of your mouths, but only what is helpful for building others up according to their needs, that it may benefit those who listen." When you tease, let it be to compliment a good quality rather than call attention to a painful one.

5. *Savor compliments.* When friends and caring adults compliment you, believe it. A good compliment can bring joy for weeks. If nothing you do stops the teasing, remind yourself that you aren't responsible for everything that happens to you. You can't control other people's choices, but you can make your own choices to bring love, not pain.

The Point: Refuse to let lonely-in-a-crowd feelings make you quit trying. Instead, let God help you recognize groups in which you could never feel at home, groups where it takes time to feel at home but are worth the work, and groups that can make you feel instantly accepted. Then work to create happiness in crowds, both for yourself and the others who want closeness.

■

Think It Through

1. Recall a time you were lonely in a crowd. What were the circumstances? The personalities? What did you do? What do you wish you had done?

2. How does focusing on others help you become comfortable? Is it possible to focus too much on others? How and why?

3. How does God guide your group friendships? How do your group friendships help you feel at home with God?

4. When is feeling lonely-in-a-crowd good? (For example, when the crowd does wrong.)

5. What's the first thing you do when you enter a roomful of people? What else might you do to make yourself and other people comfortable?

6. What relationship or conversation in your life needs rehearsal to make it go better? Practice that now.

7. Who have you hurt with sarcasm and cuts?

■

3

When I Finally Make a Friend, We End Up Fighting

"Larry wanted to get me into trouble—he deliberately knocked the report out of my hand and stepped on it."

■

"Gretta's late again. She just loves to make me mad like this."

■

"My girlfriend, Nancy, has been cheating on me. She talks to other guys just to make me jealous."

Some friends are vindictive. Some go for revenge. Some are so selfish that they think only of themselves. But most friendship problems come from accident, busyness, misinterpretation, or desire to protect one's own territory. Larry, Gretta, and Nancy didn't deliberately hurt their friends. Larry bumped Nelson by mistake. Gretta tried to cram too much into her day. Nancy talked to the other guys as friends, not as possible dates. If their friends had just talked with them, they would have realized that no harm was meant.

When you and your friend run into problems, don't attack each other. Instead, work together to attack the problem. Find the reason for the problem and a solution that pleases you both. As you and your friend talk, treating each other with consideration and trust, you can solve your friendship problems.

■

Confronting a Friend

How do I bring up a problem with a friend without getting him mad at me? Last week I asked Brian if we couldn't alternate days for driving to school rather than my doing all the driving and all the gas buying. He took my request for help as a personal attack.

There's no action that guarantees your friend won't get mad, but several actions decrease the chance of it:

1. *Be direct.* Don't expect Brian to read your mind. If he doesn't know you're running out of money for gas, he can't help

you solve your problem. Because he may already sense your uneasiness, be honest. Try words like: "I've been running out of gas money and wonder if we could trade rides rather than my driving every day. Do you think you could get a car every other day or even two days a week?" Stop and listen. It could be that Brian knows he can't get the car and is embarrassed about it. Instead of telling you this, he may call you selfish and tightfisted. In response, you may feel furious with him for using you. Move to your next response: Stay cool.

2. *Stay cool.* Rather than react, ponder what Brian's reactions and words may mean. Remember that he may have reasons he hesitates to tell. Calmly explain that you simply don't have enough money to drive every day.

3. *Listen.* Ask for Brian's ideas. If you go into the discussion with your mind made up about exactly what needs doing, Brian will be defensive. Invite him to work with you: "What do you think we should do?" "How would you solve this if you were in my shoes?"

4. *List alternatives.* List together every possible solution, including walking or riding the bus (horror of horrors!). Even the craziest ideas can lead to something that makes great sense.

5. *Go out of your way to solve the problem.* At the same time, don't give in so much that you resent Brian. There's a big difference between being cooperative and being used. If you decide to drive because Brian hesitates, you'll become angry with him for using you as a free taxi service. Look for solutions that both solve your problem and show consideration of Brian.

6. *Choose a solution together.* After you list alternatives, choose one you both like. You may decide to stop driving altogether, not for spite but to keep Brian from being jealous of your car, to save money, and to show you're willing to do whatever needs doing.

7. *Don't ignore the problem.* Ignoring the problem won't solve it. Problems seldom go away on their own. In fact, they usually get worse. Love your friend enough to work things out. The best friends are those who can solve their problems, not those that don't have any.

■

Taking a Risk

Every time a friend gets mad at me, I assume it's the end. I'm so afraid of losing a friend that I do whatever they say, or I apologize all over myself. When Trudy asks me where I want to go I just say, "Whatever you want to do." I don't want to take the risk of her not liking my choice.

I repeat: The best friends are those who solve their disagreements, not those who have none. Friendships grow with give and take, sharing and receiving, agreeing and disagreeing. During these processes you'll grow closer to some and apart from others. You fear that Trudy will grow apart from you. She may. But more likely, the two of you will grow closer as you share yourself, your ideas, your hopes, and your dreams.

True friendship takes risks. If you don't tell Trudy your feelings, ideas, and opinions, she will never learn to love the real you. To force yourself to take the risks necessary to build good friendships, realize what can happen if you don't: Trudy may get tired of making all the decisions and drop you. More friendships end when a person refuses to share than when a friend does share. Give Trudy the honest sharing you crave from her.

Disagreements give you the opportunity to grow closer. Any time there is more than one person there will be disagreements. Disagreements don't mean you aren't friends. They mean you're human. Negotiate your disagreements with actions like:

- Do what Trudy wants to do one time and what you want the next time.

- Take turns explaining the reasons you like a certain choice. Choose a third option that satisfies these reasons.

- Notice that you agree more than you disagree.

- Listen to each other until you understand.

You may feel like you need to apologize all the time because you don't believe you or your ideas are valuable. That just isn't true. God made you lovable. As you believe in and develop your God-given lovableness, Trudy and others will love you. To help you believe in yourself, notice at least one adult—parent, grandparent, or teacher—who likes you, and accept the encouragement they give you.

You are a unique and wonderful creation of God. As you learn to love friends the way God loves you, you'll develop strong friendships.

■

Give and Take

My friend Jim does all the talking and never listens to me. How can I get him to give me a chance? I want to hear his ideas, but sometimes I feel like he would be just as happy talking to a wall.

The best friendships have mutual give and take. Talk to Jim about your frustration and desire to share your ideas. Explain that he is important enough to you that you want him to know how you

---

feel. Sharing the reason for the problem as well as the problem itself will help him understand. Consider why:

THIS
IS BETTER THAN
THIS

"I want you to know how I feel because you're important to me."

"Why don't you ever listen to me?"

THIS
IS BETTER THAN
THIS

"Can we take turns telling what we have to say?"

"Will you just shut up for once and let me talk?"

THIS
IS BETTER THAN
THIS

"I'm glad you feel so comfortable talking to me. I feel good talking with you too. Can we take turns?"

"Quit taking advantage of me by yakking away. Give me a chance too!"

If you speak honestly and compassionately, you'll solve this and many other friendship problems.

■

Practical Jokes

Friday night we were out having fun, and we decided to egg Jake's house and car. It was great fun and we made a total mess. Today Jake won't speak to us. He says his dad made

---

him clean up all the egg and blames him for it. Jake's even more angry because some of the egg didn't come off. It's just a little practical joke—why does he have to get so upset?

Practical jokes are great—when they're practical. The first week I taught teenagers at my new church in Virginia, the group rolled (T.P.ed) my house. They made me feel right at home. The next Sunday they asked if rolling a house is a sin. I said, "No, unless it rains. Then it's always a sin." The practicality of a joke depends on the damage that's done. Materials like eggs, shaving cream, and shoe polish cause lasting damage. Instead of bringing a smile, practical jokes with permanent materials bring hours of work and pain.

A practical joke is practical when it brings greater closeness, not when it offends. Your joke went too far. Instead of making Jake feel loved, you made him spend his entire Saturday cleaning up his house and car. A better idea would have been to spell a huge "we love you" with forks in his yard. All Jake has to do then is pull out forks; he doesn't have to spend all day scrubbing them off. Even better would be to show up the next morning to take a picture of the masterpiece and then help pull forks.

Practical jokes should show love. Too often we do them for spite and then say, "Just kidding. Why do you take it so hard?" Be honest with your jokes. Were you really angry with Jake? Use jokes only when you care, not to get someone back for something you're angry about. Your motive will help you choose materials that bring togetherness, not pain.

■

Lying for a Friend

Jenny wants to spend the night at my house and then go out with Jason. If her parents call, she wants me to say she's at my house. I said I didn't think that would be right. She says her parents are unfair for not letting her date Jason. She said if I was a true friend, I would do it for her.

Who says a true friend is one who does whatever another friend asks? Your friendship has reached the point where loyalty ends and using begins (see chapter 6 for more on "users"). Jenny doesn't want to hurt you, her parents, or Jason. She just wants what she wants. But in the process everyone will get hurt. You'll get hurt because Jenny is using your friendship. Jason will get hurt because he can't care for Jenny openly. Jenny's parents will be hurt because Jenny will withdraw from them, worried that they'll find out what she did.

Explain to Jenny that you can't do it because sneaking is just not right. Offer to help solve the problem another way. Jenny won't take this calmly. She'll be angry because she's disappointed that she can't see Jason, she feels guilty, or she wants you to do what she's asked. But her anger is her problem, not yours. Still, don't write her off or blame her for any division between you. Just let her fume without snapping back at her.

For the sake of your friendship, do what's right. If you help Jenny sneak out she may be grateful, but more likely she'll use you again. She'll also respect you less, be less honest with her parents, and be involved in a devious relationship with Jason.

Find other ways to help Jenny get what she wants—a good relationship with parents and a boyfriend who cares. Offer to talk with her parents about Jason, and ask for the reasons why they don't want her to date Jason. Don't let using, lying, or deception ruin your friendship. By insisting on honesty, you help Jenny build strong relationships with family and friends.

■

Dealing with Cut-Downs

I can't depend on my friend—she turns on me. The other day we were talking with a couple of really popular people. Everything was going great until one of them started making fun of my sweater. He said he was just kidding, but it hurt anyway. Then my friend said, "You're right—it is an ugly sweater. I can't believe you wore it!—just kidding!" How could she turn on me like that?

Your friend probably feels as bad about what she did as you do. She may not have realized how it would affect you. And at that moment she was more concerned about impressing the popular kids than caring about your feelings.

Like your friend, we all do and say what we think the in-group wants us to do and say—it's a crazy game, but we all play it sometimes. This doesn't make it right, but it does make it understandable.

The crazy part about the game is the in-group is playing it

too. They're doing and saying what they think others want them to do and say. So nobody ends up being the person he or she wants to be and everyone stays lonely.

I don't know how to stop the game, but I do know ways to keep from playing:

1. *Think.* "But I didn't think it would hurt you!" Exactly—you didn't think. You're not immune to the pressure that made your friend hurt you. Consciously think about your words before they come out of your mouth, and you'll prevent a lot of pain.

2. *Talk.* Sometime when you're alone, talk to your friend. Say something like, "This is hard for me to say, but I was really hurt yesterday when you criticized my sweater. I guess you may have said it to impress Will. You've talked a lot about wanting to be in his group. Can you help me understand?"

Your words do three things: (1) they let your friend know she's important to you; (2) they tell her why you feel hurt; and (3) they offer a possible explanation while inviting her to explain.

3. *Listen.* Put yourself in your friend's shoes and try to understand her feelings. If your friend stomps away, let her go and

talk to her after she's calmed down. If your friend offers an explanation you aren't sure you believe, listen anyway. If your friend says something cruel, don't respond with cruelty. Listen and then say something like, "Please don't hurt me anymore. Let's work together on this."

If your friend continues to cut you down even when you treat her well, you may need to separate yourself from her for a while and find friends who treat you with the respect that friends deserve. Whatever happens, don't just let yourself be cut down. You can "turn the other cheek" without letting yourself be abused (see chapter 6).

■

Fair-Weather Friend

I am like that fair-weather friend. I know the hierarchy is wrong, but I can't help being controlled by it. I'm friendly with everyone when I'm alone. But when certain people are around I talk to just the "right" people and ignore the others. Why do I act the way I don't want to act?

The apostle Paul asked that very same question. In Romans 7:15–8:2 we see him struggling with sin. But in Romans 8:2, 9 he gives the solution to the problem: "Through Christ Jesus the law of the Spirit of life set me free from the law of sin and death. . . . You, however, are controlled not by the sinful nature but by the Spirit, if the Spirit of God lives in you." You can give control to God's Spirit and have his incredible power at your disposal.

Using God's power begins by deliberately doing what you know is right. Ask the Holy Spirit to guide you, motivate you, and give you the words. Recognize the pressure to do and say what others do and say. The hierarchy at school isn't right, but it is powerful. Know this ahead of time and pray for the power to say loving words and do loving actions, no matter who's around. Notice situations that encourage you to act cruelly or people who make you feel dumb for being you. Then stay away from those people and situations.

When you can't avoid them, pray for God's strength to be caring no matter who's around (Philippians 4:19). We all want and need friends who like us as we are, who understand us, and who encourage us to be the best we can be.

Finally, if you choose your own words and actions, you will show an inner strength that people will be drawn to. You may be criticized, but not for long and not by many. When people discover you intend to choose for yourself, they won't hassle you. Be your own friendly self to increase the chance of finding and keeping real friends.

■

Friendly Fights

My friend and I fight all the time. She's got to have her way and when she doesn't get it she throws a tantrum. She yells and leaves in a huff. Do our fights mean we shouldn't be friends?

It depends on what I call "fight indicators." The first fight indicator is the frequency of fighting. If your friend's outbursts are occasional, there is hope for your friendship. But if you find yourself constantly attacked, you probably need to develop other friendships. That doesn't mean you drop your first friend; it means you hang around with other people more often.

The second fight indicator is the type of fights you have. If you differ over matters of opinion, you can work things out. If you squabble over whether to go bowling or roller skating, you can compromise. But if you're fighting over moral issues such as lying, drinking, or cheating, there's no room for compromise. You must stand up for what is right.

A third fight indicator is the reason for your fights. If your friend seems to pick fights for no good reason, that's a bad sign. It sounds like your friend is fighting because she feels insecure and wants to control you. Your friend wants it her way or no way at all, and she thinks that if you disagree with her you don't like her.

To help your friend feel more secure try phrases like: "I like your idea but I'd like to do this too"; "That makes sense. What do you think about this instead?"; or "Why don't we do that for a little while and then try this?" Words like these affirm your friend's idea while encouraging her to listen to yours. Little by little, your friend may learn to trust you.

A measure of friendship trouble is normal. All friends disagree from time to time. We're all human, are sometimes selfish, and fail each other occasionally. Is your friend sad? Hurt? Tired? Frustrated? Confused? These feelings can make your friend fight. But if your friend fights all the time for no good reason about crucial issues, it may be time to move on. If your friend can't solve problems, find someone who can.

■

Troubled Friends

My friend drinks and does other dangerous things. She knows it's wrong. I think she just needs a little encouragement. I can be a good influence on her.

This attitude is admirable and important. A loyal friend has often helped someone do the right thing. But watch the way you help your friend. Certain settings make it nearly impossible to be a good influence—like a party where people drink. At that kind of party, the presence of a few people who don't drink isn't likely to stop everyone else from drinking. Instead, take your friend to an alternative party—a party where people enjoy each other without getting drunk, where there is an upbeat atmosphere, and where people have fun being who they are.

As you help your troubled friend, grow close friendships with other people who share your commitment to what's right. You're right to want to encourage, but you can't do it without some encouragement of your own.

■

When a Friend Moves Away

My best friend moved away, and I have no one to talk to. My mom says to make new friends, but that seems disloyal to my friend who moved away.

Separation from someone special is very painful. But take comfort: the pain doesn't last forever. You'll begin to feel more at home with the people you're around, and one day you'll be with your friend in heaven, where there are no more separations. In the meantime, God has promised, in Philippians 4:19, to meet all our needs. That includes the need for friendship. When a friend moves away, that friend remains special, but you can't talk to her as often. God provides other friends to meet your need for daily talking and listening, advice, and companionship.

Even when you don't feel like it, go places and do things with groups. Smile and speak to everyone, even people who don't initially appeal to you. Go out of your way to talk to people, and notice ones you feel comfortable with. Spend more and more time with them, and you will begin to see friendships develop.

While you're making new friends, keep in touch with your friend who moved away. Call her on Saturdays or Sundays when the long-distance rates are lowest. Write letters and send cards or small gifts that remind you of her. Send cassette tapes when you're in the mood for a long chat (you may feel funny talking to a tape recorder, but your friend will enjoy hearing your voice).

You'll discover that long-distance friendships have special joys as well. Distance makes it easier for you to confide certain problems and secrets. You'll be less competitive. And you'll be more objective.

Friendship with your old friend doesn't have to suffer because you reach out to other friends. There's room in your heart (and hers) for both old friends and new. When you worry about being disloyal to your friend or when her new friends make you jealous, remind yourself that no other friendship can replace the one you had. You both still need each other, and you both need day-to-day friends to fulfill day-to-day needs.

The Point: Discover ways to fight your problems, not your friends. With the help of your friends you can reduce loneliness and build a love that lasts. By choosing your words and actions, by solving problems directly, and by loving the way you want to be loved, you increase the chances of finding and keeping friends.

■

Think It Through

1. What do you think causes most friendship problems?

2. What scares you most about friendship problems: your friend will drop you, your friend will get mad at you, or your friend won't understand the problem?

3. How have you hurt a friend? How did your friend let you know?

4. When have you used a friend? When has a friend used (or tried to use) you? What's the best way to keep a friend from using you?

5. What makes friends turn on each other?

6. What is the hierarchy like in your school? How do you respond to it?

7. Are fights with your friend healthy or destructive? How can you make them more healthy?

8. How do you keep up relationships with friends who have moved away?

■

4

The Cliques Are Horrible at School and Church

Remember the blanket you dragged with you everywhere when you were little? You clung to it because it gave you security. Cliques are like that "security blanket." They help you answer the questions, "Where do I belong?" "Who likes me?" "What group will accept me?"

A loving, close group can make you feel like you belong without being "cliquish" and leaving anyone out. But it takes hard work to build that kind of group. It begins with being friendly to everyone and noticing their needs. It's scary to reach out, but you'll feel more secure if you include others than if you're in the most popular clique at school.

■

Dealing with Cliques

The cliques are terrible at school. Cheerleaders and jocks make up one group. Class cutters and troublemakers form another. The brains make a third group. There are even several "nobody" groups. Why can't we all get along? Why do we talk to one group and hate the rest?

We all want to feel loved. So we do almost anything to belong somewhere. We even badmouth groups that won't include us because we feel hurt by their exclusion.

Don't get me wrong. Friendship groups are not bad. They can give you support and self-confidence. They give you the security of belonging and allow you to forget yourself and reach out to others. But when a friendship group becomes exclusive, then it's a clique.

How can you build a friendship group that won't become a clique? Begin by noticing how cliques start:

1. *Some cliques form to fight a common enemy.* Some cliques hate jocks. Some can't stand geeks. Others think the druggies are the worst. By cutting other cliques down, your clique builds itself up. Listen to the names people use. Notice how names become unfair labels which separate people into groups.

2. *Some cliques grow out of insecurity.* You fear a new person would threaten your place in the clique. What if the group likes her better than you? What if they call her instead? What if she's smarter, cuter, and richer than you? Excluding everyone new protects your place.

3. *Cliques develop between people who have common interests.* These cliques form easily. A soccer player would rather talk to another player about a recent game than explain it to someone who has never played. If you're a good student, you'll enjoy hanging out with other good students. Cliques based on common interests are the least dangerous because they encourage instead of reject.

4. *Cliques occur with cheerleaders, sports heroes, and class officers because these people are more visible.* They appear in front of the school and get their names in the paper. They may be insecure, but no one knows or believes it. They get put on a pedestal and are often "lonely at the top."

5. *Cliques can form in reaction to popular cliques.* Jess and a few friends formed this type of clique. They wore out-of-style clothes, refused to please people, and insisted their actions hurt no one. Instead of using their frustration with other cliques to become accepting of others, they rejected others by forming their own clique.

6. *Some cliques grow out of anger and pain.* Andy is in an angry, class-cutting, drug-abusing, trouble-causing clique. He's angry with himself and the world because he is not as quick or as smart as other kids. Others are mad at their parents for not giving them attention and love. The reasons for their anger are valid, but their solutions fail.

7. *Many cliques grow by accident or misinterpretation.* Paula talked to Kim constantly. They never ran out of stories to tell or problems to discuss. Casey felt left out. Kim and Paula didn't mean to forget Casey. It just happened. But it still hurt.

Once you understand causes of cliques, you can keep them from forming or open already formed cliques. Do this by providing security in other ways:

1. *See people as people, not as labels.* The person you call a geek is very much like you. He too wants good friends and success in life. Instead of drawing dividing lines, notice similarities.

2. *Build security by giving it a chance to grow.* Let your friends talk to other people. You'll discover that they still like you. Free your friends to love others and open your group to others.

3. *Refuse to see others as the enemy.* Other kids at school are

fighting the same lonely battle for acceptance as you. They fear rejection and embarrassment as much as you do. Even those who are deliberately cruel may be in pain.

4. *Open your commonality clique to include whoever is there.* When a non-soccer player comes along, briefly explain the play you're discussing. Then change the subject to a topic he has experienced.

5. *Become comfortable around cliques by watching eyes.* Look into the eyes of popular people. Notice the pain and loneliness there. See that when they act tough, call attention to their clothes, or tell their latest escapade, they are begging for acceptance. Say hello and smile. Even if they never talk to you, feel better knowing they have feelings like yours.

6. *Act rather than react.* When a clique hurts you, decide not to hurt anyone else that way. Act positively. Instead of ignoring, notice people. Instead of cutting, compliment. Choose to heal instead of hurt. Get over the pain caused by clique behavior by talking to a trusted friend or adult.

7. *Admit and deal with your anger and pain.* When cliques frustrate you, get help. When your parents won't listen, find other adults who will. When life is unfair, recognize that this world is unfair—one day we'll be in heaven where there is no more crying, pain, or sadness. Ask God for real solutions that work.

8. *Overcome accidental cliques by caring.* Notice people who are alone. Invite them to join you. Reserve two person conversations for when two are alone. Give genuine compliments like: "I'm glad you're here." "Your hair looks great!" Remind yourself that you can encourage acceptance instead of exclusion.

Cliquishness is another word for selfishness. It's focusing on yourself and your group for your own sake. Help cliques vanish by looking beyond yourself to welcoming others with genuine love.

■

When You're Different

I have a lot of trouble at school because I'm different. I'm not as cute or outgoing as everyone else, and people don't like me as quickly. Some people say I put myself down too much, but they don't understand. What's wrong with me? Why am I so lonely?

Looking around at school can give you a false picture. You see many smiling faces and little pain. Behind those smiles is a loneliness similar to yours. I've never talked to anyone who feels totally accepted at school. A few feel fully accepted in their families. These lucky ones handle the school struggle better, but they still feel it.

The solution begins with taking a good look at yourself. Agony over not fitting in may stem from simple selfishness. While the self-centeredness of shyness is rarely intentional, it can be damaging. In your pain you reason, "If I felt better, I'd try reaching out to others. As soon as my pain is over, I'll notice others. I want to, but I just can't right now." Reread this response. Notice who is predominant—"I" and "my." Turning to others can ease your pain; it's not reserved for when your pain is gone.

It's not easy to face, but your focus on yourself could be preventing you from noticing others' needs. It may have begun when you got attention by complaining. You complained again to get more attention. The more you fussed, the more people pampered you. Eventually they got tired of doing all the giving and withdrew. Nothing kills a friendship faster than chronic complaining. We all need to talk about problems—the key is to take turns.

What's the solution? Change the focus of your life. Instead of focusing on yourself and expecting everyone to meet your needs, focus on God and how he wants life to operate. Let God help your feelings of shyness become less powerful than your desire to do his will. You're part of his plan. Let him equip you to trust him and care about others. Do this for two reasons: (1) others need you and (2) caring for others is what you need to do to feel included.

Make yourself listen to someone else's problem, even when you'd rather talk. Notice another's struggle to be accepted. Invite people to sit with you. Invite people to come along to the event you're attending. Look around to keep anyone from standing alone. As you focus on others, you'll forget your loneliness and discover your lovableness.

You need that deep feeling of belonging that comes when you are understood and loved for who you are. It won't happen instantly, but it *will* happen. Remind yourself often that because God made you precious you are lovable. As you care about others, you'll attract loving friends. You'll fit. Don't let your fear that people don't want you keep you from being friendly.

■

Breaking into Cliques

It's exciting being at the new school, but I don't know many people. Almost everyone already seems to be in a group, and I'm having to go everywhere by myself. How can I break into the cliques and make some new friends?

The best way to make new friends is to spend time with new people. School is a great place for that because you have so many group activities. A new school gives an advantage because many other people are new and trying to find friends. To make friends:

- Ask a classmate to meet you before school to study for the quiz.

- Invite someone who seems to be alone to sit with you at lunch.

- Compliment the person who sits next to you on a new haircut, a performance in the play, or something she's wearing.

- Observe people who talk about their faith in Christ and ask what church they go to. If they don't go, invite them to your church.

- Smile and say hi to people who sit around you in classes. Use talking times.

It becomes easier to make the first move when you realize that other people are also lonely and insecure. You may assume they don't really want to talk to you, but in most cases they welcome your attention. People love genuine compliments, genuine interest, and the friend who gives them. As with any skill, friend-making practice makes perfect.

■

Being Yourself

It really bugs me that you have to be in one group or the other. Why can't I be a little smart, a little popular, a little wild, a little independent, and a little athletic? It seems like you have to decide who you are before you can discover where you fit. Is it really possible to just see people as people?

I think so. It's not easy, but it's both possible and worth the work. The key to opening up cliques is individual friendship. As you link with people from different groups, you form a web that connects all the groups. I encourage you to try it.

You show great insight by wanting to be a bit of several good things. You can do it by making your own choices and following through with them. Although you have popular friends who cheat, decide to be smart by not doing so. Although you're smart, decide to play a sport after school rather than studying night and day. Although you're on a team and in a close friendship group, stay home sometimes to work alone. You're wise to choose happiness by deciding to be involved in several areas.

In addition to making wise choices, be yourself around

---

everyone. Treat the smart, popular, wild, independent, and athletic with the same love. You may have one friend that brings out the athletic side of you and one that brings out the academic side. That's great—each friend enhances you in a personal and important way. Do the same for them.

■

Money and Cliques

I think the clique problem centers on money. You're judged by your clothes, your car, your house, and neighborhood. If you can afford designer labels and $100 tennis shoes, you're in.

I'm afraid you're right. Teens have learned from adults how to measure people by their wealth. You know money can't make you happy, but you still feel out of it when you wear the wrong brand of shoes or jeans. Once you admit this struggle, you're on your way to solving it. No matter how much money you have, you can not depend on material possessions.

Once you've decided not to depend on material things, notice where the pressure to buy expensive clothes and cars comes from—business people. These adults use slick advertising to sell low cost items at large profits. They manipulate you to get themselves rich. Don't buy an item just because it promises to make you cute and popular. If you like it, buy it; but if you can get the same thing cheaper, do so. You can choose for yourself what to wear. Don't let someone else tell you what to do.

Even if you're determined to go against the flow, it takes only one person to make you feel out of it. The key word is *feel*. Feeling weird, ugly, or rejected doesn't mean you *are* any of these things. Your feeling has little to do with your worth as a person, or even with how others see you. People pay the most attention to their own clothes. When they do notice your clothes, it's usually to evaluate their own wardrobe. You cannot let others dictate your value. God, who created you precious and irreplaceable, is the source of your value.

This is an excellent time to depend on a friend—the two of you can fight possession pressure together. Just like a single person can make you feel worthless, a single friend can make you feel valuable. As Ecclesiastes 4:12 says, "Though one may be overpowered, two can defend themselves."

In addition to looking differently at your spending, look at people differently. Look past clothes and possessions to personality. Like God, look at the inner person instead of the outer appearance (1 Samuel 16:7). As you change your focus, you'll see yourself differently. Seeing the value in other people makes your own value more apparent. Liking people for who they are will free you to like yourself.

Finally, use your money well. Though you may not have much money, the way you spend it affects what is produced. Divide your spending by giving ten percent to church, ten percent to savings, and the remaining eighty percent for personal needs. You might use twenty percent for mall walking, twenty percent for clothes, twenty percent for church trips, and twenty percent for other expenses. When the percents are small, be creative: Use the mall more for meeting friends than for spending. Find inexpensive shops. Put your eighty percent toward one thing one week and another the next. Do without certain things.

Don't get sucked into the trap of earning to spend. This lets money control you. The Bible says, "For the love of money is a root of all kinds of evil. Some people, eager for money, have wandered from the faith and pierced themselves with many griefs" (1 Timothy 6:10). These griefs include desire for what you don't have, greed, feeling inferior to those with money, valuing people and things for their wealth, and even exhaustion from trying to work while going to school. Use money wisely rather than letting it use you.

■

Crossing Clique Lines

I try to talk to everyone, but somebody always gets mad. They say I'm disloyal and that I don't know how to pick and stay with friends. Some friends don't say anything but just quit hanging around me. Why can't people accept me when I try to cross clique lines?

Anger usually means another emotion is hiding underneath. It's hard to tell why your friends are reacting this way. Perhaps it's:

1. *Jealousy.* Your freedom to talk to people makes them wish for the same thing. Instead of following in your footsteps they accuse you of disloyalty.

2. *Fear.* One of your friends may find security in your friendship. Your making other friends makes him fear you will like him less.

3. *Guilt.* Your behavior points out their snobbishness. Instead of changing, they attack you. While they're focused on you, they don't have to face their guilt.

4. *Loss of control.* You and your friends may have built a secure little world. Your friendliness to outsiders ruins everything. Little do they know that love is a greater power than control through exclusion.

Your friends probably don't realize these things are going on inside them. Don't say, "You're just jealous." Ask them how they feel: "Why are you so mad?" Show you appreciate them by doing things with them. Maybe you could introduce them to your new friends. Explain: "These friends can make our group even better."

■

Comfortable in a Clique

You say so much about talking to everyone. I agree with that part, but isn't it okay to be closer to some than others? I have more in common with certain people who make it easier for me to be myself.

You've hit the nail on the head. Friendship groups ease loneliness. The best groups are those that encourage you to be yourself, understand you, listen to you, welcome new people, let you make mistakes, and act in ways which honor God. Such groups will be honest and compassionate, taking time for each other and reaching out to others without fear. God recommends belonging to a group that loves like he loves: the church (Hebrews 10:24–25). Work together with other Christians to build a group where everyone is accepted and genuine love exists. Encourage each other not only at church but wherever you are.

■

The Popular Group

No matter how friendly I become, I'll never be in the popular group. The cute people get the relationships, the status, the attention. They never have to worry about being alone.

It's true that cute people get lots of attention, but I'm not convinced they are less lonely. Because membership is built on status, they have to act a certain way. This is a weak foundation for friendship. They are loved for the image they project, not for themselves. It's hard to share honestly when they know certain words and actions are expected.

You may never get into the popular group, but that doesn't mean you'll stay lonely. Instead of trying to be popular, find a caring group. Begin by making one friend that brings out your good side. Do things with this friend and get to know her friends. Gradually a friendship group will grow. As you become friends with others, be accepting, caring, and honest. Expect genuineness, joy, honesty, encouragement, Christian living. Insist on friends who cross barriers instead of building them.

■

The Only Christian at School

I feel like I'm the only Christian at my school. Those who say they believe in God don't show it. Beer parties and seeing how far they can get with a girl are their main interests. Even the ones that stay fairly straight gossip and put people down. Do God's ways not work?

Yes, God's ways work. They prevent pain and bring pleasure. They solve problems. Because no one seems to agree with you, you wonder if you are wrong. You're not. If you can find just one other Christian at your school who acts out his faith, you'll feel less lonely. Your confidence in God and his ways will multiply.

God our creator knows the best ways to happiness. Disobedience to God brings either immediate or future pain. This truth does not change. Despite their popularity, some actions bring more pain than pleasure. Beer parties actually prevent closeness because everyone is most concerned with impressing each other. Using girls sexually brings a physical thrill but causes emotional pain. It can also transmit deadly diseases. Cutting people down and using them as the brunt of jokes hurts not only the victims, but also the tellers and hearers. Nobody means to hurt anyone, but it happens anyway. Meaning well won't make actions hurt less.

You've noticed the tendency to imitate the ones you're around. Even though you (and most of the others) know what you're doing is wrong, you find yourself thinking and doing as the group does. This tendency is the reason God encourages fellowship with other Christians. Look for other Christian friends. Ecclesiastes 4:12 explains the power one or two friends can provide: "Though one may be overpowered, two can defend themselves. A cord of three strands is not quickly broken." Don't ignore non-Christians, but let your closest friends be obedient Christians.

■

Church Cliques

The cliques are horrible at school and I've come to expect that. What bothers me are the cliques at church. There you'd think we could forget our differences and get along. Instead we have a group of the super-spiritual, a group who go to everything, and a group of us who are tolerated but not included. If Jesus erases all differences, why can't we get along?

Jesus doesn't erase differences—he builds bridges across them. The problems occur when people won't work with him. Being in a church doesn't make people loving Christians any more than being in a garage would make them all cars. Everyone must choose to love. People usually don't mean to be cliquish at church, but cliques still happen. Let's look at what you can do about the two cliques you mentioned: the kids who go to everything, and the super-spiritual.

1. *The kids who go to everything.* You naturally grow close to those with whom you spend the most time. The kids who go to all the events and meetings have a lot to talk about. If you weren't at the event, you may feel left out. You can do several things about this:

- Go to Bible studies and church mission events more often.

- When you can't go, listen to other kids' stories. Let them know you are interested in what the group is doing, even if you sometimes can't attend the event. And don't feel bad when you can't attend—that does not make you any less spiritual than the other kids who were able to go.

- Invite other friends along to keep you company. "Not having a friend" is the main reason young people don't get more involved at church.

2. *The super-spiritual kids.* There are always two sides to every clique problem: (1) how you see cliquish people and (2) how the cliquish people see themselves.

Those you see as "super-spiritual" may be a lot like you inside even though they are in leadership roles. Those who see themselves as super-spiritual actually may be more spiritually mature, or they may be finding their security in their spirituality. Others may have good intentions but snobbish actions (like the Pharisees and Sadducees in the Bible). The "super-spiritual" are probably more like you than not. To deal with them:

- Look for ways you are alike.

- Avoid labeling. Labels divide people.

- Be friendly to put them at ease.

- If they don't respond, try again. Even people who seem confident may need time to work up the courage to talk.

- If they still ignore you, talk to someone else. There are many people who want genuine friendship. As you make friends with the super-spiritual and others, your youth group will gain unity.

Now what about you and the others in your group who feel tolerated but not included? Being left out hurts. Sometimes your feelings of isolation are imaginary—you feel isolated when you are actually accepted and loved. Other times you are excluded. Be nice to people who reject you, but don't invest much time in them. Notice and work on friendships with people who *do* accept you.

Preventing cliques at church begins with friendliness. One or two friendly people can make a difference in the tone of the entire group. When you and a friend become friendly and welcoming, you can change your group. Become and stay friendly.

The Point: Cliques can be accidental ("I didn't mean to ignore him. I was just busy talking."), status oriented ("I have the coolest jeans."), or spiteful ("Don't talk to them. They're geeks."). Overcome these things and learn to love people for who they are, not what group they're in.

■

Think It Through

1. Choose a word that means the same as clique (samples: barrier, loneliness-launcher). How does the word make cliques more vivid? What's the difference between a clique and a healthy friendship group?

2. Around whom and in what situations do you feel like you fit? Like you don't? How would focusing on God help?

3. What makes school a friendly place for you? A lonely place? What actions can you take to make school more friendly than lonely?

4. Why do cliques happen? What's the most effective way to end them?

5. What clique at your school seems to have the most power? How did this group get that power? How is the power of Christ's love stronger?

6. Making others feel included can solve cliques. How do you do this? How do you cross clique lines? Who needs your attention right now?

7. How does money create cliques? Fund them?

8. How do cliques affect your church? How can you lessen the impact?

9. Evaluate the group of friends with whom you spend the most time. What good characteristics do they have? Destructive ones? What can you do to make your group welcoming and encouraging instead of cold and discouraging?

■

5

When Will I Be Loved?

We dream of the perfect someone who will love us forever, keeping loneliness away. This healthy desire for a companion makes our bodies and minds to do crazy things. We freeze when a special person walks into the room. We are attracted to someone with whom we have nothing in common. We ignore trusted friends' warnings of heartbreak. We put on an act to win another's affection.

The importance of romance causes much of this craziness—if it weren't serious, it wouldn't bother us. Hormones, which cause physical response to the opposite sex, cause a lot of this craziness. Even an intense fear of loneliness contributes—we'll do anything to prevent loneliness.

We start to think a boyfriend or girlfriend will solve all our problems. But it's not that easy. The solution begins by recognizing that God loves us and cares about each detail of our lives. As we find happiness in God, he can guide us to people who can love us and be loved by us. He will help us wait patiently.

■

What Girls Like in Guys

I'm sitting at home while everyone else is out on dates. How can I get girls to like me? I hear advice to just relax and be friendly, but that's not easy. If I relax too much I act stupid. If I work too hard, I look macho or scare girls away. They seem to sense my desperateness and it turns them off.

It may comfort you to know that on a given night, most people don't have dates. Relax—you aren't alone! But if you really want to go out on a date, take action.

The first step to having a good romantic relationship is to put God first. What does God have to do with romance? Consider this: There are two intense desires in every person's life. The first is the desire for God, and the second is the God-given desire for the opposite sex. Both are important and connected, but one must be first. When you put God first, he can fill your need for a romantic relationship. If you put romance first, romance cannot fill your need for God, nor can romance alone give you a happy relationship.

Keep first things first. Don't let your desire for a romantic relationship take priority. God loves you and only through him can you find happiness. Follow his guidance to be happy in dating (or waiting for dating).

God, who is love itself, wants to help you find love and companionship. Matthew 6:33 says, "Seek first his kingdom and his righteousness, and all these things will be given to you as well." Too often we focus on the "seek God first" part and fail to notice the "all these things will be given" part. This verse is a promise from a caring God. "These things" include the beginning and the building of relationships. Friendships and romances may not happen immediately, but they *will* happen.

The second step to happiness in relationships is to believe you are worthwhile. If you don't like yourself, others can't like you either. Read Psalm 139 to discover the source of your value. God made you a wonderful person—he doesn't make junk. Accept and show the good God has put in you.

Finally, love people the way God loves you. This will help others see your God-given value, help you see others' God-given value, and help you and others relax enough to enjoy each other. One of the best ways to show love for girls is to be interested in them instead of worrying about what they think of you. Listen to girls, look into their eyes, and show interest. Ask questions and remember what they say. Compliment them. Build friendship by asking about homework, attending their sports practices, inviting them along to church and school events, and sharing little things. As you practice other-centeredness with every girl you know (even moms and sisters), it will become easier with the special girls.

As you concentrate on other people, you'll forget yourself, and you'll relax. As you relax, you'll be your likable self. Love is a skill. As with all skills, the more you practice the better you become.

Girls complain: "There are no decent guys. They all care more about themselves and their macho images than about God or me. Most would rather use my body than get to know me. Why can't guys admit that they have feelings too?" Respond to their complaints by behaving like a decent person and learning to love as God does.

■

What Guys Like in Girls

Because I'm a girl the previous question doesn't apply to me. What about guys? What do they like in girls?

When it comes to being loved, there isn't a lot of difference between the sexes. Guys and girls are people first. So the three basics of loving work for girls too: Put God first, believe you are lovable, and treat people well.

Specifically, guys want girls who are honest, who like them for who they are instead of what they look like, and who enjoy sharing ideas and doing things together. Sincerity ranks as top priority in romance. Different guys want different things in girls, just like you differ from other girls in what you want from a guy. The best tip I can offer is to be yourself. Share your ideas and thoughts honestly; no one can love you if they don't know you. Let me give you an example.

"Were you planning to go to the game Friday night?" David asked Del. He wanted to invite her to the gymnastics meet, but first he wanted to find out if there was a chance she might be interested.

"Wouldn't miss it," answered Del, not wanting to admit she hated football and loved gymnastics.

"Who do you hope wins?" asked David, disappointed that Del was just like the rest of the football crowd.

You don't discover guys who like you when you aren't honest. Find kindred souls by being yourself.

When you're not dating, you may feel like a total reject. Fortunately your feelings don't match reality. You are an attractive, interesting person. The cute guy who you think will solve all your problems may be a jerk. Wait until you find someone who appreciates you. It may feel like this will never happen, but when the time is right, God will provide the right guy.

Let me repeat the importance of putting God first and choosing guys who do the same. Why? Security in God's love allows you to relax and get to know each other. The common ground of faith is a good basis for understanding. Experiencing God's great love teaches us how to love.

■

Talking to the Opposite Sex

I do okay if I'm talking to another girl, but if it's a guy, especially one I like, I get all shy and weird. One time I hid under the table and was embarrassed the rest of the night (I'm still embarrassed every time I remember it).

The more you like someone, the harder it is to talk to him. It works the other way too—if someone is uneasy talking with you or very quiet, he may be interested in you. In fact, many guys ask their second favorite for a date first to avoid rejection by their first choice. Once again, practice is the key.

Practice talking with guys you already know. The more

people you get to know, the easier you'll find relationships. Then work on feeling comfortable with the guys you're attracted to. It's rare to be totally comfortable, but the more relaxed you are the less you'll blunder and the better you'll be able to get to know the other person.

Letting the guy know you care can break the ice. Use words like these to show you care:

- "I'm glad you came."

- "You look good tonight."

- "Can I get you a piece of pizza while I'm up?"

- "Do you want to join our table?"

- "Want to ride in our car back to the church?"

Be creative in the indirect ways you let the opposite sex know you like them. Do things that give them a chance to notice without embarrassing you if they don't. Teens gave these examples:

- "I smile and look right into his eyes."

- "I ask for help with homework or if we can work together on a project."

- "I find ways to do things together at school, church, wherever we see each other. I try to get in the same study group, walk down the same hall, sit at the same table."

- "I take walks past her house."

- "I invite him and his friends to come as a group to an event I'm attending. Then we can talk casually. A group invitation makes me less nervous."

When Will I Be Loved?   **75**

The best romances are based on becoming increasingly comfortable with each other. Take every opportunity to talk together, to show interest, to become more comfortable and honest.

■

Waiting to Date

I've never been out on a date. I'm reasonably intelligent, have friends of both sexes, and try to make interesting conversation. It must be because I'm ugly or boring or won't put out. It makes me feel desperate enough to do almost anything to get a date.

Look at the people who are dating. They range from highly attractive to average to ugly. Their personalities also vary. Why some date and others don't is a mystery I don't fully understand. Some of the kindest people are not dating. This hurts because they should also experience loving and being loved. These people have much to give and would enjoy receiving as well.

Your predicament is painful but normal. The one you like doesn't like you, and the one you don't care about likes you. You've not yet found mutual attraction, and it's hard to wait. Remember that God is as interested, or more, in your dating life as you are. He will bring you love when the time is right. If you date someone you don't like or change your personality to suit another, you may get dates. But your loneliness will stay because the people you date won't like or know *you*. They'll know only the image you're projecting. It's worth waiting until you find someone you really like. If you're involved when the right one comes along, he may not notice you, nor you him.

Don't focus on the wait. Enjoy getting to know as many people as you can; this is good dating practice. Ask questions that invite people to talk about themselves. Listen well, being caring in your responses to others. Smile. Compliment others and help them feel good about themselves. Encourage them in their faith. This makes you interesting and attractive. Solve problems instead of making them worse.

As you get to know people, notice what you do and don't like in a relationship. What do you most need? Why are these things important? Do you value comfortable conversation, mutual encouragement, talking about your faith, and caring problem-solving? If you don't find friends with these qualities immediately, keep looking. Develop these things in yourself. Often when you quit seeking romance, it finds you.

And when you look for dates, remember that "opposites attract" applies better to magnets than romances. Opposites may fascinate you, but when opposite people get together, they don't tend to get along well or stay together.

■

Love or Friendship?

We've been friends for years and now I find myself in love with her—I'm so confused. She counseled me through romance problems, and I tutored her in geometry. I worked for her brother, and she taught my sister baseball. We talk about everything and have great fun together. Is it love or friendship?

Probably a little of both. The best romances are built on friendship. Being friends means you already know and understand each other, are comfortable together, and have a lot in common. You avoid much of the nervousness that strains romantic relationships. You may feel a bit nervous now that things have changed, but your prior friendship will lessen the uneasiness.

Many people are wary of friendships turning romantic because a break-up can ruin the friendship. Be honest with each other to lessen this risk. If you feel one is becoming more involved than the other, say so. Talk to understand each other. Talk about how you feel about the important things in life—God, your relationship, work, friendship, children, families, death, laughter, free time, church, and more. Enjoy little things together; even yard work can be romantic when you work with someone you love. This is loving—talking, understanding, spending time together, caring for each other.

Is it friendship or love? Don't feel pressure to name it one or the other; keep getting to know each other and enjoying each other. You won't have to decide until you're ready to marry. True love is commitment, and commitment is marriage. Decide if you want to spend the rest of your life with her. Who better to spend life with than a friend? Marriage is friendship first of all. It's sharing the daily responsibilities of decision making, paying bills, working, relaxing. This sharing is love, romance, and friendship at its best.

■

Dating a Non-Christian

I'm a committed Christian and plan on marrying a Christian. My problem is that every time I go out with someone who's not a Christian, my mom or my Sunday school teacher gets upset. I don't see why people make such a big deal about who you date. Sure, I want to marry a Christian, but I don't see why it matters now. We're just having a good time together.

A lifestyle based on God gives people the strongest basis for good romance. God, the best lover, shows us how to build love. Why wait until marriage to enjoy that? As 2 Corinthians 6:14–15 suggests, find close friends and dates who have much in common with you, who encourage you to do right, who bring happiness to your life. This is important not only for marriage, but for now.

You may agree that dating Christians is best. You would love to date someone who is interesting, cute, and Christian. But what do you do when there are none around? Can't you settle for a non-Christian? The problem here is that you get attached to those you date. Then you think you will win him for Christ. This may sound good, but usually the opposite happens—the unbeliever wins the believer away from Christ. Second Corinthians 6:14–15 says, "Do not be yoked together with unbelievers. For what do righteousness and wickedness have in common? . . . What does a believer have in common with an unbeliever?"

When you date you either break up or get married. Since you don't plan on marrying a Christian, why start a relationship that must end? Dating a Christian means a relationship could work out for life. If there are no interesting Christians around right now, wait. If you're dating someone when a cute, interesting Christian comes along, you might miss each other.

Let me add one caution, however: "Christian" is not the only qualification. Some Christians are inconsiderate, don't match your personality, or don't live their faith. Let a person's beliefs be the first qualification, but not the only qualification by which you choose.

■

Fear of Dating

As soon as somebody starts liking me I back off. Greg and I went to a movie, held hands, and snuggled. It was so romantic. On the way home he kissed me in the back seat (we were double-dating). I was pleased and scared. As the intensity increased I didn't know what to do, so I pretended to fall asleep. I know that was stupid, and I'm afraid I hurt him badly. Also, each time we're together for very long, I find some reason to go home. Then I miss him when he's gone. The more somebody likes me, the more I back off. The very thing I want, I back away from. What's wrong with me?

You're struggling with fear of intimacy—spiritual, emotional, and personal closeness. Intimacy is what makes you feel totally loved and understood. It allows you to bare your soul to someone and still be loved. Intimacy is a process of sharing that takes a lifetime to learn. You long for it because it is part of unconditional love. You fear it because the more Greg knows of you, the greater the chance he will find something he doesn't like. The more you get to know him, the more you might find that you don't like. You think: "If Greg really knew me, he'd hate me, so I won't let him get too close." Or, "He must not be worth much because good guys never like me." Intimacy requires trust and self-worth. How do you build that trust?

1. *Tell yourself you are worth knowing and loving.* You are a valuable child of God. You have a unique personality and unique gifts. You are a treasure. If you believe this, you'll believe others can like you. You won't sabotage relationships.

2. *Take relationships slowly and carefully.* True love doesn't happen at first sight, nor in a few short weeks. It takes steady sharing and honesty. Instead of deciding right off whether you are in love, let things grow. Our society forces quick decisions—"Are you going together yet?" "How serious is it?" Don't let these questions push you into something you're not ready for.

3. *Limit time together.* This is hard because when you like someone you want to spend every moment together. But setting limits is better than enduring the pressure of constantly being together. Being together all the time forces you to decide, relate, and respond much faster than you might like. Everyone, even married couples, needs time apart. You will both care more for each other if you are free to have other friends.

4. *Congratulate yourself on not rushing into physical intimacy.* You're smart to not touch too much too fast. Falling asleep may not be the best way to stop the touching, but it's better than going too far. Many couples find it so easy to be physically close that they spend no time talking and learning about each other.

5. *Share your ideas, dreams, and viewpoints.* You can't develop friendship if you act only in ways that you think Greg wants you to act. Share your thoughts; listen to his. Get to know each other. This is what love is.

6. *When someone backs off from you, don't automatically assume he doesn't like you.* He may be having the same trouble you are—he may find it hard to let you know how much he cares. Give him another chance. He may be playing hard to get because of his fear of intimacy.

■

Sex and Love

I have the opposite problem. I accepted the love of Hugh, my boyfriend, freely. He showered me with jewelry, flowers, and other gifts. He sent romantic cards and called every week at the exact time of our first date. I loved the gifts and special moments but would trade them all for a little love. They just didn't take away my loneliness. I needed someone to talk to, listen to, share with. I finally gave in to his begging for sex, hoping that would be the missing element to complete our love. His physical affection was intoxicating and we had sex for several months. Yesterday, he broke up with me, saying he wanted to date other people. I gave it all and I still have nothing. In fact, he took a part of me with him.

You've learned the painful way that sex and love are not the same. Sex expresses love but can never bring love. I don't know Hugh's motives. He could have done all the gift-giving and sweet-talking to get you in bed with him. He may not have known how to grow close so he gave things instead of friendship. Maybe he was not interested in lifelong closeness, but wanted a physical

Why Does Everybody Hate Me?

relationship. Maybe he wanted love and thought he'd find it in sex. When that didn't work, he looked elsewhere.

Whatever the reason, you feel like a part of you has been ripped away. Sex is like that. It links you powerfully to the person you share it with. Many equate its strong unifying force with love. But sex's unifying force works only inside a commitment. Outside the marriage commitment, sex leads to the pain of separation, not the joy of oneness.

How did you get yourself into this mess? You knew something was missing because you were still lonely despite all the outward signs of love. You and Hugh didn't have the genuine person-to-person sharing and support that takes away loneliness. Because Hugh's loving words were tied to physical moments, you thought that love must come through sex, so that's where you looked for it.

Now you know why sex is kept for marriage. All you wanted was a little love, but all you got was a lot of pain. You gave yourself to someone and he left you. Sex without the commitment of marriage may feel good for a while, but in the end it will only hurt you.

What can you do now? You can't physically become a virgin now, but you can be forgiven. Ask for and feel God's forgiveness. First John 1:9 says, "If we confess our sins, he is faithful and just and will forgive us our sins and purify us from all unrighteousness." God will forgive you and cleanse you. You can start again. Forgive yourself—sometimes that's the hardest part—and move on. Don't class yourself as "used" or "damaged goods." You have made a mistake, but it doesn't doom your future. You can't erase the past, but a fresh start is possible. Let it happen.

Ask God to keep you from further sin. When you're sad, angry, and hurt, you're vulnerable to falling into the same trap, to believing promises like, "He hurt you, but I won't." You may also fall into the belief that you're worthless and undeserving of a good relationship. Believe in your value as God's creation. At the same time, don't jump quickly into another relationship. Let new romances develop gradually and save sex for your wedding night.

In your anger, you're vulnerable to sins of revenge, gossip, and hate. Hurting Hugh back can never take away your pain. Don't let your anger make you bitter or cynical.

In your pain, you're vulnerable to the sin of believing that what you do doesn't matter anymore—now that you're no longer a virgin, you might as well have sex with anyone who asks. Don't fall for that temptation. God, who created you good, has forgiven you and wants you to strive toward goodness. You can't change the past, but you can change the present and future.

Finally, ask God and others to help you heal. It's easier to talk about forgiveness than it is to feel and live it. Talk with an adult you trust to help work through your feelings and affirm your forgiveness. It can help to confess to another person as well as to God.

Your situation can be redeemed. Love yourself and your future mate enough to do so. You can participate in committed, honest love.

■

Waiting Until Marriage

Our situation is about sex and loneliness too, but we love each other and won't hurt each other. We plan to get married. Ann ends my loneliness and makes me complete. Our problem is we still have a year of high school and four years of college before we can marry. How can we wait that long to fully express our love? Why would God ask us to wait that long for sex?

You don't have to wait to express your love, because sex is not the only way to express it. You say Ann ends your loneliness and makes you feel complete—how has she done this? Has she understood you, listened to you, laughed with you, enjoyed you? Continue to deepen experiences like these. These expressions and affirmations of love need not wait.

The problem of sexual expression remains. Your struggle is a tough one but can be won as you and Ann pray for strength together. People, not God, made a society that requires so much schooling that there is a ten or more year gap from the time your bodies are ready for sex until you're financially ready for marriage. In Bible times people married near puberty. Was it easier? In many ways, yes. Waiting wasn't as hard. In other ways, no. You were still tempted to sleep with those you were not married to. And once you married you needed patience if your spouse was at war, out of town, or sick. Sexual control never has been and never will be easy. God's laws applied then, and they apply now.

Why bother to obey God's laws? They work. Why control your sexual feelings? Because power is most constructive when it is controlled. Fire in a fireplace is constructive heat. Outside the fireplace, in the forest, fire is devastating. In the same way, sex as controlled in a marriage relationship is warming and constructive, while outside of marriage sex can rage out of control, burning all those it touches.

You have two choices in your relationship with Ann:

1. *You can get married now.* The finances and timing make this choice difficult. You would have both the responsibilities of school and of paying the rent and bills. If birth control fails, you would add the responsibility of caring for a child. Are you ready for these responsibilities?

2. *You can keep from hurting each other by working together to wait for sex until marriage.* Spend your sexual energy deepening the love you've begun. Love is a lifetime adventure. Like any adventure there are rough and easy climbs. As you make it through the rough climb of waiting for sex, you'll develop skills for other rough climbs. You can do it.

■

How to Break Up

I feel like I need to break up with my boyfriend, but I don't want to hurt his feelings. Wouldn't it be better to just back off slowly?

Breaking up hurts no matter how you do it. Because there's no way to avoid the pain, do the least painful thing and be direct. Arrange to get together (don't use the phone) and talk. Because both of you will feel sad, choose a time when neither of you has to see anyone afterwards.

Be direct, but gentle, telling him the reasons you want to break up. To make the breakup less painful, tell him reasons you're glad you dated. Let him respond. Listen. Understand. Let yourself cry. Accept his tears. Pray. Avoid saying: "Let's be friends"—it's hard to move immediately to friendship after being romantically involved.

Don't be surprised if you hurt too. You'll miss him even if the breakup is right. You might want to agree not to date each other for at least a month. This gives you time to tell whether you're just lonely, or if it is God's will that you get together and work things out.

■

Surviving a Breakup

I've just gone through a breakup. I feel numb, shaky, and desperately lonely. I can't concentrate. I'm angry and hurt. I want revenge. At the same time, I'm grateful for the time we had and I see why we broke up. Why is all the love I felt turning to hate? If we cared why are we breaking up? Wasn't it love to begin with? What should I do?

Your love is turning into hate so you can protect yourself. If you can say you hate her, you don't have to admit your pain over losing her. Love also turns into hate because both are intense emotions. No one can hurt you unless you care. I'm glad you're honest with your feelings. Many hide their hurt, insisting "She didn't hurt me!" Being honest helps you heal.

Your numbness and lack of concentration result from the intense mental anguish you're feeling. You can only feel so much pain. The mind protects itself by turning off the feeling circuits while it adjusts. You don't feel joy, interest, hunger—anything!

Your anger and spite are loneliness turned outward. You want to be loved. If you get angry enough about the breakup, maybe it will go away. This makes no sense, but anger isn't logical. You must feel pain in order to heal. Feel your anger and pain. Pray about your feelings and share them with a friend. They will slowly disappear. The Bible says to be angry without sin (Ephesians 4:26). Don't let anger lead to revenge, slander, or worse. Ask your family and friends to listen to your hurt and love you through it.

Your confusion may result from declaring the relationship dead. You're angry because it's over. You're confused because you two were so happy for a while. Feel both things. Don't try to unite them. A breakup means the good has ended, not that there was nothing good to begin with. Don't let a breakup block what you taught each other or the good you brought out in each other. Remember the love, not the pain.

A breakup is complex but important. You must heal well to be ready for future relationships. Think about what caused the breakup. Was it caused by incompatibility (as most are), something you did or didn't do, or something she did or didn't do? Learn from your mistakes. What personality characteristics did and did not match yours? Review the relationship until you feel free to go on. The longer you dated, the longer this will take. In the meantime, don't jump into another romantic relationship. Instead surround yourself with family members and friends. Read Bible verses that give you hope, like Jeremiah 29:11: "'For I know the plans I have for you,' declares the LORD, 'Plans to prosper you and not to harm you, plans to give you hope and a future.'" Let family, friends, and God love you as you heal.

The Point: Finding a girlfriend or boyfriend seems the best solution to loneliness. But it's not that easy. The best boyfriends and girlfriends are happy before they meet each other. Instead of finding your security in others, find your security in God so you can be free to love others. Set out on the adventure of friendship building.

■

Think It Through

1. What do you struggle with most: wishing you had someone to get close to, fear of getting close, or getting too close too fast? How can security in God's love help you with each of these?

2. What advice can you give for dealing with loneliness while not dating?

3. Why is friendship the best basis for romance? If romance comes first, how might you strengthen the friendship?

4. Why is it important to date Christians for now? For later?

5. How are love and intimacy different from sex? How does loneliness make you vulnerable to sexual involvement? What can you do about it?

6. Name several ways to express love besides sex. Why should you wait until marriage for sex, even if you truly love each other?

7. How do you control relationships? Give too much control to the other? How does control keep love from growing? What might God suggest to make a relationship more mutual?

8. What signals the need for a breakup? What words and actions make it easier to do the breaking up? To recover from breaking up?

■

6

My Dates and Friends Are Using Me

Things are mixed up. Instead of using things and loving people, we use people and love things. Why do we treat people as if we didn't care about them? Perhaps because we are afraid of getting too close. To protect ourselves from getting hurt, we act like we can take care of ourselves. We hide our loneliness and try to fill it with material things. When things fail us, we try relationships, but instead of taking chances and letting a friendship grow, we pull back. This causes the very rejection and disappointment we fear.

Why don't we grow close to people? Why do we use people instead of loving them? Because love is hard. Loving friends and family is one of the hardest tasks in life. But it's worth it. To begin, decide to love people no matter how much work it is. Depend on God's power to enable you to love. You will discover that as you reach out to others in love, God will fill you with joy and take away your lonely feelings.

■

Users

Guys are such users. Why can't they just drop the macho act and admit that they need people too? Is there any way to stop using?

Old habits are hard to break. Some guys were pressured into using girls by their friends, while others learned to use from their dads, who learned it from *their* dads. But don't accuse only guys. Girls can be users too. Using people has more to do with selfishness than gender.

A person uses others when he or she considers only his or her own needs. He uses someone as *his* date to the banquet and then drops her. She uses someone to make *her* ex-boyfriend jealous. He uses someone to do *his* homework. She uses someone to get *herself* into a group. Using stops when you consider other people's feelings.

Some people are users because they're scared of getting close. More people are users because they've done it before and it worked. They think, "Why not use people if it gets me what I want?"

Because using continues when people get away with it, don't let it happen. Don't let people continually borrow money without returning it, copy your homework papers, or always get a ride with you. Explain that you can't loan more money until you are repaid. Point out to your friend that without doing his homework he won't learn the material for the test. Offer to trade rides. Not letting yourself be used and explaining why will help your friends learn to love unselfishly.

Refusing to be used is more complicated when it occurs in a

relationship. Relationships develop best on trust, and trust is what users abuse to get what they want. Trust, but don't trust blindly. Trust gradually, and only as you see evidence of trustworthiness. Take a second look if a boy asks you out, but ignores you at school. Your date may be shy—or you may be getting used. Ask him about it: "Why haven't you talked to me since you asked me out?" Listen carefully to his answer and decide what to do. You can't keep people from trying to use you, but you can keep them from *continuing* to use you. Give them a fair chance, but don't stay friends with someone who uses you or anyone else.

The second way to stop using is to not use. Consider others' feelings as well as yours. Treat others with kindness, making them feel better about themselves, not worse. Be genuine and honest. Every word you say can either build someone up or tear them down. Build people up; don't use them.

■

Turning the Other Cheek

Jesus said to turn the other cheek, so I don't get mad when I get used.

There's a difference between turning the other cheek and letting yourself be used. To turn the other cheek (Matthew 5:39) does not mean to ignore evil, but to respond to it with actions that diminish it. Turning the other cheek means not returning evil for evil, because retaliation only increases evil. However, ignoring evil lets it continue. Turning the other cheek is finding a third way to respond to insult or injury, a way that stops evil.

When you let someone use you, you encourage him or her to keep using you and causing you pain. By letting someone use you, you are throwing your pearls—your value as a person—before pigs (Matthew 7:6). Jesus did not let others use him. Rather, he constantly frustrated evil by doing good. You can do the same by responding in ways that decrease using.

Find out whether you are turning the other cheek or letting yourself be used by considering the effect of your action on the user. If he becomes more considerate and caring, you are probably turning the other cheek. If he becomes more selfish and demanding, you may be encouraging instead of stopping evil.

There's a fine line between serving and being used. Practice distinguishing the two with these examples:

It's service when...	It can be using when...
A group gets together to do an invalid's chores.	A friend coerces you to do her chores so she can go to the ball game.
You stick with a friend until she overcomes her shyness.	You put up with a friend's selfishness instead of insisting on give and take.
You buy a friend's pizza because she forgot her money.	You always pay your friend's way because she knows you will.

Remember: Turning the other cheek means to respond in a loving way, a way that is good and healthy for both you and the person who hurt you.

■

When Dates Use You

Dates seem more interested in using my body than loving me. I know sex is wrong, but if I don't put out, I'll be lonely. Isn't second-rate affection better than nothing?

I understand your fear of loneliness, but I don't agree that second-rate affection is better than none. If you refuse to let people use you, you will be less lonely than if you continue to have sex with dates. If you continue, you'll feel even more isolated and deserted. Letting people use you sexually makes you feel second-rate. Then you don't even try for a good relationship, because you don't feel like you deserve one.

In spite of your feelings, you deserve quality relationships. Love yourself enough to protect yourself from being used. Sex does not equal love. You already know the pain of rejection after having given everything. Sex without commitment in a marriage brings pain, not fulfillment.

Sex is an expression of committed love. It is not love itself. You know this, but have a hard time believing it, because sex feels so good. You hear loving words and have loving feelings. Television and magazines support your feelings with the message "Sex is love." The media show only the pleasure, not the loneliness and pain that may result from sex. No painful consequences are shown. Sex outside marriage is painful and uncertain. You're afraid you'll lose your relationship if you don't have sex, but it seems to drive you apart instead of together.

All you want is to be loved. That's a good desire. Find love by dating guys who like your personality and not just your body. Those who demand sex would probably break up sooner or later whether they got it or not. When you're not dating, focus on friendships with both sexes. Be warm and caring, listening with interest. You will be attractive if you are genuine.

If you treat people well, they'll do the same. Kindness and honesty build good relationships. They anticipate sex in marriage and prevent the use of sex as power. Sex is sacred and beautiful if it is saved for marriage. If you're risking sex to find love, it shows you are desperate for love. Use that desperation to seek lasting love. It will take time to develop healthy relationships, and it won't be easy, but relationships based on love rather than sex will last. This is much better than second-rate "love."

■

When Dates Want to Be Used

I don't want to use people, but there are some girls who practically throw themselves at me. If they're offering sex and we're using birth control, why is it wrong? If I'm giving them what they want, isn't that okay?

Would you let a baby play with a poisonous snake because she thought it was pretty? Of course not. You'd think about what was best for the baby. The girls who throw themselves at you want a love relationship, not a body-only relationship. They may think sex is love because it gets you involved with them. They think if they give you sex, you will give them love.

Is that what you're giving? It doesn't sound like it. Even if you did care about the girl, sex outside marriage is destructive. It separates instead of uniting. It is a very personal experience, a complete sharing of yourself. It can't be love when it's casual.

It's never okay to use someone, even if they offer it. If you like one of the girls, go out with her, but don't have sex with her. Show her the care she craves non-physically. It will be more sincere, more romantic. As your relationship grows, let kisses and hugs show love, but keep sex for marriage. It's not only smart, it's more loving.

■

Knowing
When to Trust

I've been used in the past, and I don't think I can ever trust again. Everything about this girl seemed sincere, but she used me and dropped me. How can I keep from being so stupid again? How can I know when to trust and when to be suspicious? How can I tell if somebody really cares?

That's a tough but important question. The best answer is to go s-l-o-w. Trust is important for a solid relationship, but it shouldn't blind you. A painful relationship makes you vulnerable to a rebound relationship. You want desperately to believe the person who says, "She treated you like dirt, but I never will." This vulnerability leaves you open to being used again. Trust is necessary for love, but it must grow gradually based on actions. True caring is active. Does she say she cares, but cut you down in front of her friends? Does she compliment you? Does she listen to your ideas with interest? Talk is cheap. Caring actions are a sign of real friendship. When you open yourself slightly and she treats you well, open yourself a little more.

Listen to what friends say. What do they know about the way she has treated others? How do they see the way she treats you? Filter out gossip and jealousy to find concerned comments.

You're wise to be cautious. Don't date for a while. Consider staying friends with a girl for at least a month before going out. If you find someone you're interested in, build a friendship first. You may want to explain that you've recently been hurt and want to go slowly. In the meantime talk on the phone, in groups, at school, whenever you see each other. Waiting can make the date more romantic when it comes.

■

Building Trust

What do I do when I hurt someone I care about? I took Kathy out to make Amy jealous after we broke up. Amy wasn't jealous, but Kathy got hurt. While I was out with Kathy, I discovered that I really like her. But she knows I used her. How can I get her to trust me again?

You've learned the hard way that using people causes more pain than pleasure. Trust, not jealousy, is the sign of a good relationship. You've broken trust with both Kathy and Amy. To mend the situation you'll need to talk to both girls because they're both important and because each may tell the other what you say.

Talk to Amy. Apologize for using someone else to convey

your hurt. Tell her what you felt (you wanted to stay together) and how you feel (you know you can't stay together and are glad for the time you had—and that you are sorry you used Kathy). Ask for forgiveness.

Go see Kathy. Begin by saying you know you have hurt her. Then apologize and explain. Say something like, "I know I was wrong. I was so hurt when Amy broke up with me that all I could think about was my own feelings. I used you to make her jealous. There was nothing right about that. Then when you and I went out, I realized I like you. I know you probably don't feel like forgiving me or trusting me. But I ask you for both. I wasn't honest before, but I'm being very honest now.(Be certain you are!) Can you give me another chance? It doesn't have to be right away, because I know I hurt you badly. But after you've had some time to heal, would you consider going out with me again? Right now, all I ask for is forgiveness."

If Kathy does go out with you again, be totally honest. Tell her when you feel like you might be tempted to use her or someone else. It'll take time to build trust, but it is possible. Take it slow and easy and be very honest along the way.

Risking Rejection

I keep from being used by avoiding people. People can't put me down if I don't spend time with them. No one can reject me if I don't ask them out. Nobody can break up with me if I don't get involved.

Keeping to yourself means you'll never get hurt directly. But you'll be hurt by the continual pain of loneliness. There is no closeness without risk of rejection. The pain of loneliness is greater than the pain of occasional rejection.

Your battle is real and difficult, but it can be won. It's not easy to overcome fear of rejection. It takes repeated effort to become confident and to find people who like you. Remember your God-given value. Knowing the battle is hard makes it easier to fight. Begin by turning outside yourself.

Turning outside yourself is easier when you join groups that reach out to others. Just one other person reaching out can make it easier for you to do so. A church youth group is a good possibility. Hallie joined a youth group on Saturday mornings which taught a Bible study in an area without a church. The people hungrily consumed what the group taught. The hugs of the children and smiles of the adults made Hallie feel loved and useful. Her youth pastor praised her way with people. Each positive reaction made Hallie feel better about herself and more willing to reach out.

When people show you love like people loved Hallie, it becomes easier to feel your God-given worth. But if people use you instead of loving you, does this confirm your worthlessness?

No! It only confirms that you need to find different friends. Trust friends and family members who bring out your good, who encourage you to be your best, who help you feel loved. Choose friends who are more good than harmful.

Take a look at the following examples. Which are examples of genuine love, and which are examples of using or being used?

- Dave found an accepting, loyal group. All he had to do was help them with homework and he had a place. They protected him, complimented his brains, and didn't let anyone put him down.

- Susan found the friend she needed in Stan. He built her up, cared for her, gave her courage, made her happy. He was the one Susan turned to for strength, encouragement, and approval.

- Larry found the love he'd been looking for in Linda. When his mom yelled or his out-of-state dad didn't call, Linda was always there for Larry. She opened her arms to him and took away the pain.

Let's take a closer look at each of these situations.

Dave's group was good for providing acceptance and protection. But it was hurtful because Dave's acceptance was conditional. It used Dave for his brains instead of caring for him personally. All groups have both give and take, but stay away from groups who ask more from you than they give. The exception is a group of caring Christians who spur you on toward love and good deeds and who encourage you to obey Jesus (Hebrews 10:24–25).

Stan was a great friend to Susan. He gave encouragement, support, and assurance. But he was Susan's only friend. Susan turned to one person for her all affirmation. She became so dependent on him that she couldn't get through a day without him. We all need a circle of caring friends. Within that group one or two will be special. But let more than two friends give you the support you need.

Larry turned to a physical relationship for acceptance. Sex can't make love grow or last. Only commitment, communication, and consistent caring can do this. Linda was a good friend in that she was there for Larry, but she cheated him by loving him only physically.

As you reach outside yourself to become friends with others, watch for users and notice those who care. Share your ideas. Talk honestly with caring people. Let them know you so you can find the love you need. As you struggle to make friends that won't use you, don't use others. Your care can increase their care for you.

The Point: Decrease loneliness by not using or being used. Everyone is irreplaceable and valuable. Treat everyone well, and don't let yourself be used.

■

Think It Through

1. When do you use people, or feel tempted to use them? How does paying attention to other people's feelings affect your actions?

2. How have you been used? How effective were your responses to it?

3. Compare Matthew 5:38–42 to Matthew 7:6. Both were spoken by Jesus at the same sitting. How do they affect how you respond to using?

4. What is the difference between serving and being used?

5. How would you convince a friend that he or she was being used sexually? Used another way?

6. What makes someone feel they must give sex to get or keep dates? How and why do you recommend staying a virgin?

7. Name a Christian who has the qualities you'd like in a friendship or romance. Be this way yourself. Look for people with those qualities.

8. How has God healed you or someone you know after you (they) were used? How did you (or your friend) learn to trust again? Is it possible to build trust with a person you have used or have been used by? How?

9. When we're all so lonely and need each other so much, why do we keep using each other?

■

7

My Parents Just Don't Understand

Home is supposed to be a haven, but it is often a battlefield. Even when you have supportive parents, you'll argue sometimes, and the conflict can make you feel miserable. It's hard to be at odds with those you love and depend on. Take heart. When people live together some conflict is unavoidable, for each of us has different ideas, opinions, and goals. You don't have to let those differences separate you. Face conflict head on and solve it. Share ideas, list possible solutions, and agree on a solution that works for everyone.

■

Authoritarian Parents

You've got to be kidding. There is no problem-solving in my family. My dad says do it and I do it. That's how he solves conflict.

It's easy for a parent to order his teenagers around without listening to them. Your dad sounds like an authoritarian parent. Authoritarians dictate behavior and rules, expecting obedience without back talk. They think any protest is a threat to their authority. Therefore, they allow none. Authoritarianism is dangerous because it centers on the parent, who makes all the decisions without his teenager's input. This does not teach teens how to make decisions. And you need to learn to make decisions in order to become a mature adult.

Authoritarianism is also dangerous because the parent could be wrong in his decision. Not listening can lead a parent to make an unwise decision. For example, Mr. Holms made a bad decision when he forbade Chris to go on the church canoe trip, saying it was too dangerous. Chris knew the water was only three feet deep, that life jackets were required, and that the trip was well supervised. Mr. Holms had only been on a canoe trip in rapid water without life jackets, and his best friend had almost drowned. He wouldn't listen to the facts.

Authoritarianism is easy, but not best. A parent who leads with authority but listens with understanding to the facts and opinions is better. Notice the difference: The parent still has the final say but includes God and his teenagers in the decision making process. It is easier to obey if you are included in this process.

If your parent abuses his or her authority, you may just have to take it. But there are actions that can change things. Let's look at those actions, and see how Chris could apply them to the conflict with his father, Mr. Holms.

1. *Share your ideas calmly without being defensive or demanding.* Chris could say to his dad, "I know canoeing sounds dangerous to you, but we take lessons first, and a guide goes along."

2. *Give the facts before requesting.* "Dad, there's a canoe trip this weekend. The water is three feet deep at most. We have to wear life jackets. Mr. Elliot and two sponsors are going. May I go?"

3. *Pray for your parent's decision.* "God, please help Dad to be reasonable."

4. *Pray for your parent to trust you.* "Lord, help my dad see that I'm responsible. Help me make good choices."

5. *Obey your parents to build trust.* "I really want to go, but I'll obey and stay home."

6. *Try to see the reason for your parent's decision.* "He wants me to be safe. At least he cares about me."

7. *Don't rebel; it will only make things worse.* "I could spend the night with Jo and go anyway, but he'd find out and never let me go anywhere again."

As you endure unfair or unwise decisions, try to keep a positive attitude. Remember that dealing with difficult parents will give you good practice for hard times to come. Keep trying—your efforts may change things.

■

Rules, Rules, Rules

My parents are always making up rules. If I do something good, I get a privilege. If I do something bad, I get punished. Why do they stay on me? When are they going to realize that I'm grown up and can choose for myself?

You are blessed with parents who care enough to help you learn from the consequences of your behavior. As you learn what brings good consequences, you'll act more responsibly. Too many parents quit caring, quit giving rules, and quit being involved, thinking that their teenagers don't need them or that it's too hard to discipline a teenager.

Why do you need discipline? To teach you how to live responsibly so you don't unintentionally hurt anyone. Your parents use rewards and punishments to teach you to live safely and responsibly.

When you run through the gym pushing a friend on a folding chair, you might collide with someone, causing a serious injury. You wouldn't have meant to hurt anyone, but saying you're sorry won't help. So your parents punish you by keeping you home the next weekend. This reminds you to choose fun that won't harm others.

When you mock a classmate, your parents might cut your phone time to show you that if you are going to speak cruelly, they'd rather you didn't speak at all. Cruel words can cause more painful scars than any physical injury.

Good discipline is not always negative, however. Sometimes it should be positive, rewarding you for good behavior. For example, when you show your parents you can play in the gym safely, they might let you stay later next time. And when they sense that you are trying to speak kindly about all your classmates, they may allow you to have a friend over to show you that kind actions bring friendship.

The goal of discipline is self-discipline. As you behave considerately and thoughtfully, your parents won't need to reward or punish you as much. Your own happiness and the happiness of others will be enough. Until you can be self-disciplined, you need a caring adult to guide your behavior.

You are lucky that your parents notice your good behavior as well as the bad. Ask to work with your parents to set consequences. When you help set the rules, you'll be more motivated to work with them. Rules and consequences will bring security.

■

Inconsistent Punishment

I'd love it if my parents would reward my good points. They only notice the bad. Their rules are usually reasonable, but sometimes they ground me for something I didn't know was forbidden. They're inconsistent—sometimes I get punished, sometimes I don't. How am I supposed to know what to do?

You are frustrated with your parents' rules. It bothers you that they notice only what you do wrong. That's a valid complaint. When both you and your parents are in a good mood, thank them for caring enough to punish you. Then explain that you would like them to notice your good behavior as well. Ask if they'd encourage you when you do something good. If you accept punishment graciously, your parents may encourage your good behavior more readily.

You want to know the rules ahead of time. That's usually possible, but unforeseen situations often come up. For example, you aren't allowed to drive with more than one friend in the car, but your parents haven't forbidden you to ride in a friend's crowded car, so you go along even though there are four people in the car. You get punished. Were your parents fair? Certainly. The same principle applies in both situations—a young driver doesn't need too many passengers. Maybe you and your friends go swimming at the local rock quarry. You don't have a rule against this, but your parents punish you anyway to emphasize the importance of not doing it again. Most of the time you know when something is wrong, even if you and your parents haven't discussed it. This is a chance to show your maturity. Evaluate things yourself to determine their safety so no one else has to.

Finally, your parents' inconsistency bothers you. It's no fun to get away with wrong sometimes but not others. Avoid this by behaving wisely even when no one is watching. Wrong is wrong, whether you get caught or not. When you control your own behavior, your parents won't need to. When your parents really are unfair, obey as best you can. Although this is hard, you will be doing right even in a bad situation, and it will give you practice for other unfair situations in life. When your parents are unfair, it is more their problem than yours. Ask God for wisdom and advice in this difficult situation.

■

Absent Parents

I'd love to have a fight once in a while with my mom. It would be better than constant loneliness. She works day and night, and when she gets off she's too tired to have anything to do with me. How can I depend on my mom when she's never even around?

Your loneliness seems unbearable. You wonder, "If my own mom won't take time for me, who will?" Understand that her neglect of you doesn't necessarily mean she doesn't care. She may want to spend time with you as much as you do with her. Knowing why she works can help you know what to do. Your mom may work to earn money. Encourage her with words and actions. Do some of the daily chores so that you can have some time together. Or do some of the chores together.

Your mom may love her job. You go to soccer practice not to avoid your parents, but because you love soccer. Similarly, your mom works because she enjoys her job. Ask what she likes about her job and listen to her answer. When she notices you taking an interest in her work, she'll want to talk with you about it.

Your mom's long hours may be temporary because of a new project that requires extra hours. Wait patiently for the time she'll have later.

Your mom may be working overtime to earn money to buy things you want and need. Let her know that time with her is better than any material thing she might give you. Your mom may work because she feels pressure to be productive. Spending time with you is productive, but it doesn't bring a paycheck.

Whatever the reason, ask your mom to work out some together time. Ask her when she is rested, not when she's exhausted. Fix breakfast while she gets ready and talk then. Schedule a "date." Call her at work at an agreed upon time. Finding time to spend with your parent is a tough job, but it's worthwhile. Do all you can to make it happen. If nothing works, savor the time you do have.

■

Establishing Trust

Why can't my parents trust me? They have to meet who I'm dating and know what the family is like. Then they ask where we're going, how late we'll be out, and more. Why can't they just ease up and let me have a good time?

Parents have funny ways of showing their love. They ask questions, set curfews, get to know your friends, and worry about you. This much interest from a friend might be okay, but it's different from a parent. Why? Because parents can enforce their interest.

How do you deal with this?

First, remember that most of the time your parents want the same thing you do: happiness, friends who care, and time for both work and play.

Second, remember that parents are worried that you'll get hurt. You don't plan to get hurt and they know this, but they still fear it. They may have been hurt before, may have a friend whose teenager just was hurt, or may have read an article about a teenager's pain. You are more valuable to them than their own lives. Their questions are an attempt to ensure your safety with the person and activities you've chosen. It's not you they don't trust. It's the unknown date who's taking you out or the drunk driver going your way.

Finally, give your parents the trust you want from them. Tell them why you chose the activity, why you chose to go with the person(s) you're going with, and what you'll be doing. This not only cuts down on the questioning, but also gives them confidence in you.

■

Not Another Lecture

I want to talk to my mom, but every time I try to share a problem, story, or idea, she switches into lecture mode. Why can't she listen instead of lecturing?

Nothing makes you feel lonelier than someone who won't or can't listen. I don't know why your mom doesn't listen. Perhaps:

1. *She's busy.* Perhaps she has a full-time job, two volunteer positions, and three kids (including you) to help with homework.
2. *She's tired.* By the time the two of you finally connect, it's late and she's exhausted. She wants to listen but she has no energy.
3. *She's impatient.* She wants you to see things the way she sees them, learn the way she learned, and do things the way she wants them done.
4. *She's afraid.* Parents have a tough time letting their kids make and act on decisions. They are afraid you will get hurt. Fear makes parents lecture. They think if they tell you what to do, you won't make a bad choice.
5. *She talks better than she listens.* Listening is difficult. It requires understanding, close attention, and deciding how to act on that knowledge. Not all parents have this skill.
6. *She listens but doesn't show it.* She may not know how to put her understanding into words. She may not look at you while she listens. She may speak only when she's upset.
7. *She doesn't agree.* Disagreement makes you feel she doesn't understand.
8. *She's more concerned about her needs.* Sadly, some parents are self-centered. Because of past problems or present self-focus, your mom may not want to face what you are facing, so she turns you off.

To get her to listen, ask for a time when you and she can talk. Knowing ahead of time that you'll be talking can make both of you receptive. If time is short, perhaps you can talk while you drive somewhere, while you do chores at home, or while you get ready for school.

If there is no communication between you, discuss a relatively neutral topic first. As you come to an understanding, move to more complex or personal topics. It may help to listen first to your mom. When she's felt like you've listened to her, she may be more likely to listen to you. Keep trying little by little. Listening and understanding take time.

■

Clothes War

My mom says we can't afford the clothes I want. She says less expensive clothes look just as nice and wear better. She doesn't know what I really need and she says I'm wasting money. But I've got to have nice things to wear. Why is she so against me on this?

The clothes war is constant, but it doesn't have to be violent. Your mom is not your enemy. You're actually both struggling against high prices and fashion pressures. Attack the problem together.

Notice how you both see the problem. Your mom has a set amount of money to use for the needs of every family member. You have little or no money and see mostly your own needs. Neither of you are wrong; you just see things from different points of view.

Take on some of your mom's distribution burden by doing your own clothes budgeting. Ask your mom for your portion of the clothing budget for the season (or the month so you don't blow it too fast). Then decide how to spend it. Agree on conditions, like:

- Once the money is gone, you get no more. You'll have to wait until the next season (or month) to buy more clothes.

- Unexpected expenses such as sports banquets don't (or do) count.

- Other items such as shoes, socks, and pajamas count.

- Advice or suggestions may be requested/offered by either party at any time.

By budgeting your own clothing money you can learn what you can and cannot afford. You can learn from your wise and unwise choices. You can ask for your mom's advice instead of for her money. If you want to spend more than you have, earn it. (A word of caution: don't let desire for clothes force you to work too much. Your time is valuable.) As you spend, consider these buying tips:

- Make a list of every item of clothing you need and want. Don't forget pajamas, socks, underwear, shoes, jewelry, and belts.

- Place the items in order of need and preference. You'll have to put some "boring" items such as underwear first.

- Shop before you buy. Price items to see just how much you can buy for your money. Include tax in your totals.

- If the money doesn't cover your list, find similar items at lower prices and recheck the list to see what you can do without.

- Make the most of sales.

- Keep a reserve of money to buy something new for a special occasion.

- If you have a sibling your size, share some items.

- Buy clothes that match a lot of your other clothes.

　　　　　　　Why Does Everybody Hate Me?

- If you make a mistake, figure out what you'll do differently next time.

If your mom won't let you have the money, you can still use these buying tips when you shop with her. Show that you are trying to make wise clothing choices. Work with her instead of against her to fight the cost of clothing and build a wardrobe both of you can be proud of.

■

Parental Neglect

I've tried all the things you say about getting along with parents, I really have. But my parents don't care what I do, think, or say. My mom is so concerned with what other people think that she can't make her own decisions. She's embarrassed about my hair and my clothes because she thinks the neighbors don't like them. She likes me only when I do stuff for her or give her things. I called my dad and said I wanted to stay with him for a while. He said he'd only be in for three days. I thought, "That's okay, Dad, I'm just your son." If your own mom and dad don't care, what hope is there?

Rejection by parents is deeply painful. Our parents' attitudes toward us strongly influence our self images. The bitter truth is that some parents just don't care about their children. They have chosen to focus only on themselves. Most often lack of caring is accidental. Parents often don't realize when they're neglecting you. That's when you need to show them that you care about spending time with them.

Parental neglect problems can be mild or serious. Some parents just misunderstand. They don't remember being teenagers with good ideas and the need for encouragement. Instead of admitting fear, they may yell at you (fear can come out as anger). They might be too strict. Such problems are discouraging, but usually with a little communication and trust, such rejections can be avoided.

The problem is more serious when your parents can't or won't express care for you. Some parents can't care because they've never felt care. Their parents didn't listen to or encourage them, and they follow this pattern without thinking. It's not fair, but knowing the reason can help you take it less personally. In your case, your mom has never felt secure in her choices. She is more worried about the neighbors' opinions than your needs. She sees you as a reflection on her, not as a separate person with important needs.

Other parents don't give the time or effort to care. This is seldom intentional—they just focus on other things. Your dad focuses on his work and travel. This keeps him from noticing your needs, feelings, or accomplishments. He has a weak relationship with you because he has no relationship with anyone but himself.

Your parents' lack of outward love seems to be a result of things that have nothing to do with you. Seeing the reason doesn't always reduce the pain, but it can make it easier to bear. It can also help you know what to do about it. Learn to share your feelings, express your needs, and negotiate solutions with your parents. These things have worked for other teens:

1. *Keep your voice calm even when your parents yell.* This keeps fights down and may increase trust.

2. *Spend a little time with each parent daily.* Write weekly to those who don't live with you. This gives space for good conversations while minimizing opportunity for fights.

3. *Find adults who affirm your worth.* They can show love by taking interest in you and taking your needs seriously. You'll find

these adults at your church in Sunday school, Bible studies, and discipleship classes.

4. *Don't repeat your parents' bad patterns.* If they shout or hide their problems, talk out yours. This will take deliberate and repeated effort but will reward you with more loving relationships.

5. *Don't let anger or apathy overtake you.* In your frustration and pain over not being loved, you may lash out at others, or you may try not to care about anyone or anything. We express anger and apathy in similar ways—by using people, denying feelings, rebelling, having sex, insulting others, alienating ourselves, and not trying. You are valuable no matter how your parents treat you. Believe this and live it.

6. *Pray.* Because Jesus was misunderstood, abused, ridiculed, and ignored, he understands you, and he knows what to do. Find a Christian to pray with and for you. Return the favor.

7. *Get support from friends.* Ask friends what they do to solve their parent problems. Share your pain and frustration. Work out solutions and encourage each other to try them. Friendships can supply the love you need to get through. However, don't depend only on your peers for love and support. Make friends with adults too.

8. *See it as your parents' problem.* As one teen says, "My mom's total unconcern for me is her problem, not mine. She has chosen to remain self-centered instead of loving me. It hurts and I wish she would change, but I can't make her. God has given me other caring people. I'll make it because I know God is at my side."

9. *Focus on your actions.* You can't change your parents' actions, but you can change your own. Talk clearly and calmly, show love, listen. Your loving actions can encourage loving response from your parents. If your parents choose differently, don't feel guilty for it.

10. *Don't run away.* If you're being abused and home is unbearable, call the Department of Human Services. Your pastor or youth group leader can connect you with other sources of help. Turn to caring adults instead of running away. Running away won't solve your problems; it will only make them worse.

It's not fair when you have to depend on yourself instead of your parents. But even in unfair situations, God is powerful. He'll give you strength to act when your parents cause you pain. He'll help you respond lovingly when your parents yell at you. If your parents don't care for you, others will. Ask God to bring these people into your life.

Some parent problems cannot be solved—some parents never learn to care for their children. This is a painful reality. If it happens to you, remember that your parents' rejection does not mean you are worthless. You *are* worth spending time with; your ideas *do* count; your feelings *are* important; your accomplishments *do* matter. Even if your parents don't respond to your efforts, God and other people will.

The Point: You're becoming more independent, but you still need a lot of support, encouragement, and advice from your parents. Talk calmly, trust patiently, and work together with your parents to solve problems.

Think It Through

1. What do your parents do that makes you feel less lonely?

2. What do you like and not like about the way your parents deal with conflict? What do you like and not like about the way you solve conflicts? How is cooperative decision making best for your family?

3. Name a rule in your house that protects you physically. Emotionally. Spiritually. Thank your parents for these rules. Name a rule you don't understand. Request an explanation, and if the rule seems unfair, talk with your parents about changing it.

4. What makes your parents notice more bad than good? More good than bad? Do you notice more good or bad in your parents?

5. Name a positive way to ask for a parent's attention.

6. Name three things you want to know about your parents. How could you find this out? How might they do the same with you?

7. When does your parent listen best and lecture least? How might you use this to minimize future lecturing? When does listening to lectures help?

8. Develop a spending plan.

9. How do your parents feel about you? How has that affected your view of yourself? How does God want to change that view?

10. Recall a time you and a parent really understood each other. What did you do and say to make this happen? What did your parent do and say? How might you repeat that understanding? Thank God for this.

11. What do you want to imitate about your parents? What do you want to do differently?

8

My Teachers Never Like My Work

School can be great or nightmarish depending upon how well you're doing in class, how well you're getting along with friends, and how interesting your classes are. Since school is your job right now and takes up most of your day, ask God to help make it pleasant. Take school seriously and learn as much as you can. If you are having trouble in school, look for ways to resolve your conflicts with teachers, or ways to improve your grades. Here are some ideas to get you started.

Teachers' Pets

I want to be a good student, but the teachers only pay attention to the smart kids. Why can't teachers like me for me, not my grades?

Many teachers do like you, but two things prevent teachers from showing how much they care: amount of paperwork and number of students. Preparing tests, grading homework, and averaging grades can take their attention from students' needs. Most teachers have at least five classes of 25–30 students. Treasure the teacher who singles you out and gives you special attention.

The smart people do get more awards and recognition, but that does not mean they are more loved. Some teachers cater to naturally smart students, but most care about all students. In fact, some care more for those who must work for their grades. To have a teacher notice you, remember:

1. *There is more than one way to be smart.* You may be smart in mathematics or in mechanical abilities. You may have great ideas and the ability to solve problems well, or you may be a terrific artist or intuitive friend. There are many areas in which you may do well. Some of the most successful people and inventors were C students. They had to study hard for those grades, demonstrating their commitment to hard work. Some people get C's because they have so many interests they weren't able to give more than average attention to each subject. While this is no reason to slack off, if a C is the best you can do, be proud of it.

2. *Teachers like cooperative students even more than brilliant ones.* Your efforts to keep discussion rolling, to care for others, to do as

the teacher asks, and to complete homework can win your teacher's heart.

3. *Teachers have different personalities just like students do.* Some will give you more recognition than others. Some will naturally "click" with you, while others won't. Be friendly to both kinds of teachers, being careful not to antagonize a teacher who rubs you the wrong way.

4. *Understand that teachers are lonely too.* As you show care for them, they tend to care for you in return.

Pray that God will bring at least one caring, supportive teacher into your life. It takes only one to convince you that you are competent and significant. Treat all your teachers well. Your kindness can prompt caring. Some call this being a teacher's pet; I prefer to think of it as treating teachers as people who need attention. It's also loving like Jesus loves.

■

Homework Overload

Everyone else seems to breeze through their homework, but my teachers load it on. Why are they against me? Why am I so stupid I can't get it done?

You are probably just overloaded, not stupid. You are not alone here. Students across the globe groan under loads of homework. The only solution is to do it. Some find it easiest to come home, eat a brief snack, and get right to the work. This keeps their evenings free for relaxing. Others choose to have a free afternoon and do homework after supper.

If you can't get your homework done with time to spare, ask for help. You may just need tips for working efficiently, or you may need help to understand the material. Your parent or older sibling might explain the material in a way that makes perfect sense. If they can't, find a friend, teacher, or tutor who can help. In addition to this, begin with the hardest subject and go on to ones that require less concentration.

If your homework load is really unfair, ask for your parents' intervention. A group of equally concerned parents can approach the teachers and work on finding a solution together.

Homework is frustrating after you've already put in a full day at school. But it's part of life. Take heart; many students struggle with you.

On the Teacher's Black List

Once you get on a teacher's bad side, he stays on your case all year. I do my best, but since my sister was smarter and I made bad grades in the past, I'm branded. I can't seem to change his mind.

Like the rest of the world, school is not always fair. Some teachers let first impressions determine how they see you the rest of the year. If you're on a teacher's good side and you get in trouble, he assumes you're just having a bad day. If you're on a teacher's bad side and get in trouble, he assumes you're working against him.

Once you're on a teacher's bad side, use your best behavior and hardest work to show you've changed. As teachers see evidence of change, they may accept you. If you never gain his confidence, remember that it's his problem, not yours. Don't become what he thinks you are—lazy, a cheater, or a troublemaker.

You might want to schedule a conference or write a letter to humbly ask the teacher to work with you and encourage you. Perhaps you can share how important it is to you to be given a fresh start. By not ignoring or explaining away the past you show your willingness to change.

If your efforts don't work, you may want to ask for help from your parents, a guidance counselor, or a principal. They can look at the situation and decide how to handle it fairly. If nothing seems to work, take heart—another year is coming and it can give you a fresh start.

■

School Rules

Why does the school have so many rules—don't they trust us?

Rules are made to increase, not decrease, trust. Imagine going to a school with no rules. You arrive at school early to find all the lockers unlocked and someone at your locker going through your stuff. When you ask what he's doing he says he needs a pencil and a history book. "But this is my locker," you say. He replies, "Too bad, I got here first." When you try to take the book away, he slams you against the wall and leaves. Frustrated, you take a book from another locker, but that owner has torn out the chapter you need. When you finally find an intact book, you begin reviewing for your test, but it's so noisy you can't concentrate. During the test people throw pencils, talk, and share answers.

A nightmarish scene, isn't it? That's why we have rules. Rules are made for your own personal, social, and physical safety. To give you security the school has rules that require locks on lockers, give guidelines for classroom talking, appoint hall monitors, and assign due dates. When rules seem silly, figure out what or who they are designed to protect.

■

Starting a New School

I'm getting ready to move from grade school to middle school, and I'm nervous about learning so many new rules and expectations. What if each teacher has different rules and I forget whose is whose? Besides that, there will be a lot of new people, and I may not know anyone in my classes.

You are expressing fear of the unknown. The changes can be hard, so it's smart to think ahead. It can help you to plan what to do to prevent the things you're worrying about. Face these changes head on, call friends, and share your fears. Because God cares about the details in your life, pray for his insight and help.

Getting used to a new school and new friends takes time. In your eagerness for instant comfort, you may feel like nothing is working. Notice each step of progress—each step adds up. Take your new school adjustments slowly; with God's power you'll make it through. Here are some things you can do to feel comfortable at school:

1. *Before school starts.* Ask to go through the building a day or two ahead to practice finding your classes. Some schools offer this during an open house. Also, ask around to see who's going to your school.

2. *The first day.* Take notes on each teacher's rules and expectations. Be friendly to teachers and students. Start conversations with the students who sit on both sides of you in classes. Good beginning questions are "Which school did you go to last year?" "What's your schedule?" "Do you have any homework yet?"

Why Does Everybody Hate Me?

When you get your locker combination, practice opening and locking it. Keep your locker combination written down but don't tell it to anyone. Even if your friend won't steal from you, a friend of a friend might.

Expect to feel tired and even a little discouraged at the end of the first day. Your energy has been sapped by so much information to absorb and so many new people to meet. You'll grow more comfortable as time goes on.

3. *The second day.* Keep taking notes in class. If it's written down, you'll have less trouble remembering. Begin a new conversation with the people you talked with yesterday, and say hello to at least one new person today.

4. *The second week.* Your schedule should be making sense by now. Thank God for the friends you're making and for other victories you've had at school. Ask God for help with things that still frustrate you. And finally, share your progress with a parent and one of your new friends.

The point: School is a group effort—you, your friends, and your teachers work together to create a meaningful and loving learning environment. Pray for guidance on how to make this happen.

■

Think It Through

1. How do you get teachers to notice you without playing up to them? How do you feel valuable even when you've failed or teachers ignore you?

2. Name at least ten ways to be smart. Which two ways are you smartest?

3. How do you get your homework done and still have free time?

4. How have your older siblings made school easier for you? Harder? How are you currently making it easier or harder for your younger siblings?

5. How do you recommend getting on a teacher's good side?

6. What advice do you have to give someone who is starting a new school?

■

9

I Don't Even Like Myself

Seven hundred fifty people packed the church for Cliff's funeral. We agonized over how much we missed him, but we agonized even more deeply that Cliff, at the age of seventeen, took his own life because he believed nobody cared about him.

Was Cliff ugly or stupid or unpopular? No, he was bright, friendly, likable, and compassionate. He had accepted Jesus and was eager to follow him as Lord. Cliff listened to problems without interrupting. He always wore a smile. His warm teasing showed how glad he was to see you. He could make an adventure out of anything, even working in a fast-food restaurant. He had all the qualities of a genuine friend. People loved him. But Cliff didn't believe it.

What made Cliff kill himself? Maybe because of his absent father, angry stepfather, or uncaring mother. Perhaps all his weekends home alone while his parents were out on the lake drove him to it. He was desperately afraid that no one cared.

Where does this fear come from? Why is liking ourselves so hard, even when people show us love? Why do we only hear the

---

cuts and deny the compliments? Why do we see ourselves as ugly when others see our beauty? Why, even when we know God made us, do we doubt our beauty, refuse others' care, and believe we are worthless? I don't know why this struggle to love ourselves is so hard, but everyone fights it at some level.

Just as surely as I know the struggle is hard, I know that we are loved. God cares for us individually and personally. I can see it in the way people care about each other. Those who struggle with liking themselves are loved dearly by people around them. God is the source of love, and he makes sure that each of us has at least one person who cares. While it may not be the parental or romantic care we want, there will be someone to care. More often, it is several someones. Cliff, who didn't believe seven people could love him, had over seven hundred people attend his funeral. No matter how painful our circumstances, God lights our darkness with love.

■

Feeling Like a Failure

Everything I do goes wrong. I tried out for the soccer team and didn't make it. I felt like a total wimp. When I worked up the courage to talk to Sarah I burped when I opened my mouth. I was so embarrassed I just walked away. I knew the answer to the question, but when the teacher called on me my mind went blank. I felt totally stupid. I guess I'm just not as smart or athletic as everyone else.

Why Does Everybody Hate Me?

Failure is enormously painful, especially when it's public. You are afraid no one will like you because everything hinges on how well you do. But your feelings don't match the facts. You're not less smart, competent, or valuable than everyone else. You had a bad day. More people get cut from the team than make it. The burp was pure nervousness. Your mind went blank.

Even when you know the facts, your feelings of hopelessness remain. What should you do? Let yourself feel sad and discouraged for a while. Share your feelings with a parent or friend. Let them encourage you without denying your sadness, and let them remind you of your worth. Feeling your sad emotions will help them to heal.

Move from sadness to hope. The failure, not your lack of worth, is why you feel hopeless and despairing. You don't have to stay down, because God is the God of hope. He always has a solution. He will help you handle failure and show you what to do next. He'll guide you to a way to use your sports talent. He wants you to have another chance to talk to Sarah. He can help you relax next time the teacher asks a question.

Take action. Perhaps you need more practice for the next tryout. For now choose a different sport or activity for the season. Return to Sarah, apologize, express your embarrassment, and ask for a fresh start. She'll be touched by your honesty and humility. And before you raise your hand to answer a question, jot down the answer so you can look at it when the teacher calls on you. If your failure doesn't provide a second chance (it was the final exam so you can't re-take the test) grieve over it. Pinpoint something you can do to keep from failing when a similar experience comes along.

You've felt your feelings. You've turned to the God of hope. You've taken action. Now affirm your worth. Ask a family member or friend to help you do this, or you may prefer to do it on your own. You are a worthwhile, valuable person created in God's image. Even after failures, you are precious.

■

Outer Beauty

I like myself fine until I look in the mirror. There I see zit pits a mile deep, hair that never lays right, and braces. The last time I babysat the kids asked me if I had the chicken pox. I was so embarrassed! How could anyone like me when they have to get past a face like mine?

You know that outer beauty is only skin deep. You know that personality makes the difference and externally beautiful people can be very shallow. And you know that everyone worries about their physical appearance, even the girls with beautiful complexions. But these facts don't help much when you're home on prom night, when someone more attractive gets the job, or when you get a big zit on your nose the night of the big date.

Unfortunately, we live in a superficial world where people judge on surface appearances. The encouraging news is that even in our surface world, looks alone can't make anything last. Guys are quick to say they want more than air inside a beautiful head. Girls despise attractive guys with manipulative personalities. Looks can be destroyed instantly in an accident or gradually by age.

Even so, you want to be attractive. A good personality is nice to have, but some good looks would help a lot. You can be attractive without changing the shape of your face or the proportions of your body. Focus on your eyes, your smile, and the ways you enhance your features. Eyes and smiles are the source of true beauty, both inner and outer. Eyes show honesty or anger, compassion or criticism. Smiles are real or fake. Notice the laughing, loving, sparkling, and teasing eyes in the people you like. See the pain caused by cruel, distant, and distracted eyes. Truly beautiful people will smile *with* people instead of *at* them. Your eyes and your smile can enhance your beauty like nothing else. Look at people with affection, understanding, admiration. Smile to show concern, care, and compassion.

Second, appreciate your own special form of outer beauty. Beauty comes in many forms: freckled and freckle-free, dark and light, curly and straight, round and square, tall and short, formal and casual, blond and brown, fancy and simple. Find at least one feature on your face and one feature on the rest of your body that you like. James says Sal's walk first attracted her to him. Her hips moved in a cute way that wasn't flirty. And as she walked she talked to people and smiled, showing her dimples. James was startled to discover Sal's walk was the very quality that made her self-conscious—one hip is higher than the other and causes her to walk awkwardly.

What do you like on your face? Is it your hair, your dimples, your teeth, your ears, your chin, your eyelashes, your nose? What do you like on the rest of your body? Are you happy with your knees, your wrists, your fingers, your shoulders, your neck, your toes, your weight (not everyone can eat whatever he wants and never gain an ounce)? When you discover even one beautiful quality, you begin to feel (and act) beautiful. Don't depend on outer beauty to win and keep friends. Do let it help you appreciate the good way God made you. Let it free you to like yourself enough to stop worrying about your looks.

To help you discover your beauty, look around at school or church. Notice the many kinds of faces and the many kinds of beauty around you. Without comparing yourself too much, notice beauty like yours. How might you enhance your beauty? What styles look best with your type of hair? What colors would look best on you? How do Rachel's freckles make you feel better about yours? Notice and enhance the features God has given you.

Finally, because mirrors can depress, look in the mirror less. Some Christians don't even allow mirrors, thinking they encourage vanity. I think they encourage sadness. No matter how attractive we are, mirrors remind us of our flaws. I can have a wonderful evening with caring friends and feel very loved and happy. Then I'll come home and look in a mirror, and my happiness and confidence will fall apart. I'm better off looking in mirrors just enough to get the food out of my teeth!

Your physical beauty is enhanced when you are genuine, easy to talk to, and interested in people. Cultivate these qualities.

■

Inner Beauty

My ugliness comes out in my thought life. I think about stuff I'm ashamed to talk about. Some of my thoughts are angry, even violent.

Most people struggle with their thoughts. Thoughts are how we deal with what we see, hear, and experience. Most thoughts, even angry ones, are ways we make sense of life. If your dad just forbade you to go to a concert, you may be furious with him and plot ways for revenge. Thinking it through helps deal with your anger and frustration. This is okay and normal. If, on the other hand, your thoughts lead you to a wrong action, like wrecking your dad's car or sneaking out to attend the concert, it's not okay. Your thoughts have led to sin instead of to resolution of the problem.

Do your thoughts work you up or calm you down? Solve the problem or make it worse? These are the questions you need to ask. When your anger leads to violent thoughts or when violent images bring you pleasure, you need help expressing your anger. You may need to work out on sports equipment, write an angry letter that you never mail, or talk to someone who can absorb your anger without becoming angry. Discover the source of your anger and what can be done about it.

Anger is a valid and important emotion designed to lead to positive action. It is like a pressure cooker—it needs a venting system or some way to turn it into good. Without a vent, it builds until it explodes and causes damage. If you can't vent your anger, ask for help from an adult who can. Your minister, youth pastor, or other Christian adult are good people to ask.

■

Dirty Thoughts

I have trouble with sexual thoughts, especially after I've been to the beach. Am I the dirtiest person on the face of this earth?

Probably not. Just as thoughts can help you work out anger, thoughts can help you work out sexuality. There's nothing wrong with sex and thoughts about sex. God created both. Romantic thoughts can give you the courage to talk to the person you like or solve a romance problem. However, romantic thoughts are bad when they become lust. Lust treats people as objects for satisfying one's own sexual desires, and if left unchecked, lustful thoughts can lead to lustful actions.

Good sexuality encourages relating to and loving people. Within marriage, sexual intercourse is one of the many things that expresses that love and relationship. Our sexuality is a good gift from a holy God. But without commitment, communication, understanding, and thoughtfulness, sex means little. Because our society delays marriage so long past the age of physical readiness, we must anticipate sex long before we experience it in marriage. This makes lust a continuing problem.

There are two creative and effective ways to handle lust. One is to talk with God about it. God is probably the last person you'd like to talk to about sex, but before you totally reject the idea, consider these facts: (1) God created sex and made it pleasant; and (2) God came to earth and lived as a man—yet never had sex. He knows how to live life and enjoy it fully without experiencing sex. He knows, both by creation and by experience, of even higher pleasures that are available to you right now. These pleasures include the understanding that erases loneliness and the joy of sharing a special time with someone you care about. God has the strength to harness the power of sex. Ask him to give you that strength.

When you talk to God about your thoughts you can't help but get them under control. Tim Stafford in his book *A Love Story* has explained that sex is more a drive that needs a steering wheel than a need that invites indulgence. God will grant you understanding, guide you toward solutions, and equip you with his power.

If you're honest, you may admit that you do not want solutions. You may want to savor your fantasies for a while. You may enjoy the feelings lust brings. This sounds okay, but these feelings lead to a lot of frustration. Limit your thought to a moment of appreciation, not an extended period of contemplation. God made bodies attractive. Thank him for that. Then move on to other thoughts. When lustful or other people-using thoughts come to mind, tell them they are not welcome. Replace them with loving thoughts—such as "Boy, she's pretty! Thanks for making such a good body, God. I hope you'll let me find that same attraction to the person I marry." As you talk about sex with God, your thoughts become good.

The second action that helps with lust is to get to know people of the opposite sex. As you talk with them and enjoy them as *people*, you have less chance to see them as *things*. Again, pray for help. Sometimes as you get to know a person, your sex drive gets stronger. This isn't lust as much as a natural desire from a good God. It becomes bad when you let it lead to action, or let it dominate the relationship. Move from lust to loving actions such as talking, sharing experiences, encouraging, and caring.

■

Crazy Thoughts

My thoughts aren't really ugly, but I sometimes think they're crazy. Late at night I wonder where I was before I was. I wonder what I'll be doing in ten years. I wonder why I fear what I fear. I'm afraid to tell anyone my feelings and confusion because they won't take them seriously. Then I'd feel real stupid. Does everyone worry this much?

Once again, thoughts are the ways you work out your feelings, fears, and questions. Honest questions aren't crazy. God wants you to understand yourself, your thoughts, and his thoughts. Daydreaming, praying, and pondering are ways to figure things out, to refresh, revive, and deepen yourself. If questions remain even after you do this, seek answers in the Bible, Christian books, and people you trust. Do this cautiously, sharing with those who will take you seriously. Sunday school teachers, youth pastors, and ministers can often answer your questions. No matter how someone responds to your questions and thoughts, they are important.

The point: When you don't like yourself, find the reason, and work toward a solution. Not liking yourself can lead you to hurt the very friends you need. Trust that God made you good and lovable, and care for others so that they too can believe in their own worth.

■

Think It Through

1. Why do you think people have trouble liking themselves? What makes it hard to love yourself? What helps you believe your God-given lovableness?

2. How have you healed after failure? Who or what helps you reaffirm your value? How might you help someone else make it through failure? (For example, help clean up the dropped lunch tray instead of laughing.)

3. What do you like about your physical appearance? Thank God for making you beautiful in this way. What nonphysical qualities enhance your beauty? What other qualities can you develop with God's help?

4. What do you think about that bothers you? How can talking to God about these thoughts transform them into something good? Help you understand? Help you feel more comfortable with yourself? With God?

■

10

I Wonder If Even God Has Rejected Me

When something tragic happens, you might think God doesn't care about you. When you've done too many things wrong, you might conclude that God won't love you. When your life is a mess, you might think that God has left you. These feelings make sense, but they don't match reality. Don't let inaccurate feelings hurt your relationship with God.

Believe that God cares, loves you personally, is always there to answer you, has the power to handle any problem, and loves you no matter what you've done or what you think. These are the facts, no matter what your feelings say. God may not like your actions, but he always likes *you*—let his love move you to please him.

■

Honest Doubts

You say God is there and he's on my side, but I can't always feel his presence. Sometimes I wonder if he is there at all or if he even cares about me. Does this mean I'm not a good Christian?

No. Honest doubts make you search out the facts for yourself. Instead of feeling bad about doubts, pursue them until you find the answers you need. God wants you to know, understand, and trust him. Doubts demand answers, and God has them. In fact, healthy doubting can keep you from getting sucked into a cult or other false religion. Doubts are bad only when you use them as excuses to stay away from God.

The disciple Thomas didn't believe Jesus had risen from the dead until he had evidence. Jesus did not condemn him for his doubts. Instead he gave Thomas the evidence he needed: nail-scarred hands and a wounded side. Thomas responded by worshiping Jesus. Like Thomas, let your doubts lead you to find answers and draw you closer to God.

God wants to give you evidence to answer your doubts. You wonder if God is real. Consider this evidence:

1. *The intricacy and complexity of the world.* Many believe the earth and its inhabitants came about by cosmic accident. But consider the earth's complexity, from flowers to people. Could such intricacy have happened without a Master Designer?

2. *People.* If we are a simple cellular progression, why aren't we all clones? Two daisies look remarkably similar, but no two human faces are alike. Why is each person unique? If we evolved

from a single cell, why can we appreciate beauty, experience pleasure, create ideas? Uniqueness and individuality point to a personal and caring Creator.

3. *Inner yearnings.* Routine life isn't enough. We want a reason to love, a reason to live, a reason to work, a reason to be. No human relationship or experience can fill this void within. Only God can do so.

4. *Science is not everything.* Many say it's impossible to prove God because he can't be seen or touched. You can't bottle, culture, dissect, or date love, friendship, or emotional pain either. But their reality is undisputed. Similar proofs point to the reality of God.

5. *Jesus.* God has come to earth in the man Jesus Christ. He was fully human and fully God. Many say he was just another religious leader, but Jesus changed the course of history. All time either points forward (B.C.) or looks back to Jesus (A.D.). Jesus claimed to be God. C. S. Lewis suggests that this claim means Jesus was either Lord, Liar, or Lunatic. What do we think about people who claim to be God today? They're either lying or crazy. If Jesus lied, he would have called off the joke before the crucifixion. If he

falsely believed he was God, he would have shown signs of mental imbalance. The only remaining option is that Jesus really is God. As Lord he has the ability to guide us daily.

6. *The Bible.* More than just another religious book, the Bible is the Word of God. It has been verified again and again by history, science, and archaeology. It has a remarkably strong sense of internal agreement for a book that was written by so many people in so many time periods. It is authentic; it is the Word of God. You can depend on what it says.

Even when you know God is there, you want to know that he cares. What if you can't feel God? How can you know his care for you? God's presence in your life does not depend on your feeling it. He's there whether you feel him there or not. The Bible confirms this.

I wish someone had told me how to deal with feelings. During the closing worship service of my fifth summer at church camp, everyone cried, hugged, and felt God's presence. At all the other services I too had felt God's presence. This time I felt nothing. I spent a month of terror fearing God had left me. I was too scared to tell anyone, but I finally found an article that calmed my worries. It explained that feelings are dependent on facts, not vice versa. The fact is: God said he would stay with us if we invite him into our lives (Revelation 3:20).

Feelings can be a powerful way to worship, but they can also be influenced by lack of sleep, what you ate for lunch, or illness. When you can't feel God, read the facts in such verses as Jeremiah 33:3; Romans 8:38–39; Matthew 28:20; John 14:18; and Psalm 103:17. Place your faith in the facts, not in your feelings.

Even when you read the evidences and the facts, you may doubt. When you fail, hurt someone, or do something really stupid, you assume no one could love you. But when you succeed, care, or make someone happy, you believe God's care because you feel deserving of it. People like you when you are good and reject you when you are bad. But God is different. No matter how you act, God still cares. The Bible repeats over and over that God cares for you because he made you. You can count on God's unending love and continuing presence. It's a fact.

Questioning God

I've heard you should never question God, but I have lots of questions. Why is it bad to ask when you want to know?

It's not. Questions become bad only when they're used as excuses for not believing or obeying. Good questions are requests for greater understanding, or for God to calm our fears. Even Jesus asked God if he might skip the crucifixion (Luke 22:42)—not because he wanted to disobey God, but because he wanted to understand.

When you have a question about math you go to someone who knows math. Similarly, when you have a question about people, about the way the world works, or about something eternal, you ask the One who created people, who knows the intricate workings of the world, who can see past time. Asking questions shows that you trust God, not that you don't. So ask on!

■

When Life Is a Mess

Last night Mom came home in a terrible mood. She yelled at me to set the table and keep Jeremy quiet for a few minutes while she grabbed a quick nap. When I turned my back Jeremy jumped on her and startled her so badly that she couldn't go back to sleep. Mom was furious with me and supper was a disaster. Then today Carl told me a story when the teacher gave the assignment and I didn't hear it. I had to catch the bus before I could ask anyone about it. Now I don't know my homework and my friends who do are in band practice all afternoon. By the time they get home, I'll be at Bible study. When I get home there won't be time to do the assignment. If God loves me, why is my life such a mess?

God's love does not mean everything will go well. Look back at the things that have happened to you. What caused them? People. Why did God allow these bad things to happen? He does so for the sake of freedom. To keep the world and its events in perfect order, God would have to control each person and event. He knows we don't want or need to be controlled. We would rather choose our own actions. Only when we choose can we truly love, and experience joy and happiness.

Sadly, the opposite is also true. Freedom of choice gives the freedom to cause pain. Your mom can take her frustration out on you instead of talking it out patiently. Your friend can choose to talk to you instead of listening to the teacher. People can use their knowledge to cure cancer or to create atomic bombs. Why does God allow this freedom? If he stopped every wrong choice, we would not be free to choose.

God grieves along with you when people choose to cause pain. It's not fair and it's not right, but it's reality. Instead of focusing on the unfairness, focus on God's power. He can help you rise above painful circumstances to find joy—that may be a greater miracle than a world without pain.

In the midst of this, you're yelling, "Yes, but I still have to face my mom tonight, and tomorrow's homework awaits!" God promises his power to meet all your needs. Philippians 4:13 says, "I can do everything through him who gives me strength" and verse 19 says, "My God will meet all your needs according to his glorious riches in Christ Jesus." Your needs include facing your mom and finding a way to get your homework done. In both cases, someone made a choice that messed up your need. No one meant to cause pain, but they did.

Once you understand the causes, you can move from frustration to solution. You can't change other people's choices, but you can change yours. Use your freedom to make things better. Understand that your mom is having a bad day, and respond with love. Don't take it personally. Go out of your way to care for her, just like she might do when you are frustrated. When she's in a good mood, tell her that it makes you sad when she yells at you. Ask if you might talk it over calmly next time.

As for your homework, call another friend and ask about the assignment. Next time a friend talks during the assignment, use your freedom to listen to the teacher instead of your friend. Lessening frustrations is not easy, but God with his unlimited power can help you do it. As you face frustrations, God is fighting with you.

Bad days don't mean God is mad. They mean we live in an imperfect world. Even more importantly, we have a God who agonizes with us, knows the solutions to our struggles, and helps us rise above our frustrations. Whether things are going great or not, God loves you and is on your side.

Suffering

I'm fighting cancer and wonder what I did to deserve it. I can't trace that back to a human choice, so it must come from God. Kids my age don't get cancer! Why did this happen to me?

You did nothing to deserve your cancer. Cancer and other illnesses are not punishment. They are a result of living in a fallen world. But why you? Why did God allow it? These agonizing questions have plagued people for generations. Begin to understand the answer by knowing that God is the giver of good gifts, not tragic ones (James 1:17). Don't blame God. He cries with you. He allows sad things, but he doesn't like them.

Tragedies and pain come from four sources: Satan, your choice, another person's choice, or an imperfect world. Let's examine each of these possibilities:

1. *Satan's action.* God doesn't give troubles as gifts, but the devil does. Recall Job, the Old Testament patriarch who suffered from horrible disease and lost his home, family, and livelihood. Satan was the source of Job's troubles, not God. Job's friends said Job must have done wrong to deserve illness and troubles. They warned Job to repent. Job disagreed and vehemently defended his innocence. He knew that God may have allowed his troubles, but he didn't cause them. Some people cut off God, the only source of power who can help, because they feel he caused their troubles. When you realize Satan is the source of trouble, you are free to invite God to fight with you. You don't have to be mad at God.

2. *Your choices.* Some cancers are caused by the victim's

actions, such as smoking or sunbathing. Your cancer is not this type. You don't have to blame yourself or God for it. Instead look at other choices and their results: If you drive over a cliff, gravity will smash you at the bottom even if you are a Christian. If you tell a secret a friend asked you not to tell, she may not trust you in the future, even if you are a Christian. God doesn't "get you" when you do wrong—instead he lets the natural course of things occur. He gives his laws ahead of time so we don't have to learn by experience. We can avoid much pain through obedience.

3. *Another's choice.* People have created disease by polluting air, water, and food. People demand products that require dangerous chemicals in production. A toxic waste transporter may have dumped near your community's water supply instead of in the approved site. An exterminator may have sprayed your house with a chemical that made both you and the bugs ill. A choice or series of choices like this may have caused your cancer. It's not fair when someone else's choice causes you pain.

4. *An imperfect world.* When Emily's cancer was diagnosed, friends told her she got cancer because she was a strong Christian and could be a good example. This sounds very spiritual, but Scripture doesn't back it up. Troubles aren't given as a reward for good behavior. They result from living in a fallen world. Birth defects, crippling childhood illnesses, viruses, earthquakes, and floods seem senseless and cruel. They have no clear cause. They are somehow part of the struggle between good and evil that plagues us and the world (Romans 8:20–22).

Once you understand a bit of the why, focus on the more important question: How will you get through this? God is the answer. He is on your side, not against you. He is your strength, not your source of pain. Ask him to walk with you, to fight with you against the cancer, to give wisdom to your doctors, to help you triumph over it. He, and only he, has the power to do this.

You have experienced suffering not because of God's anger, but because of another's choice, an attack from Satan, or our imperfect world. God is by your side to get you through it. One day, there will be no more tears, no more death, no more mourning, no more crying, no more pain (Revelation 21:4).

Sin and Forgiveness

You mentioned bad choices. I've made more than I can count. I've used people, stolen, lusted, and worse. I've done so much wrong that God could never forgive me. I guess I've sealed my fate.

You have decided that you have sinned beyond God's capacity for forgiveness. Therefore, you feel no need to try anymore. Many people share your fear. But it is false. God loves you freely, not because you can earn his love. He wants you to refrain from sin because it will bring harm, not because it will cause you to lose his love.

You may feel you have committed an unforgivable sin. Certain sins are more destructive and seem unforgivable. What might you name—murder, sex outside marriage, divorce, turning someone away from God? What about murder with words? Using friends to get a date? Fights within marriage? Gossip? Sin is sin no matter how great or small. Matthew 12:32 and Luke 12:10 make it clear that the only unforgivable sin is turning away from God. This is unforgivable because God can't forgive those who don't turn to him. If you're worried about the unforgivable sin, you probably haven't committed it. Repent (turn from your way to God's way) and ask for forgiveness.

If you can be forgiven simply by repenting, why not go on sinning and asking for forgiveness each time? Because sin causes damage. Sin is sin not because God set down arbitrary laws, but because it hurts people. Avoiding sin means avoiding pain, both yours and someone else's. You can be forgiven for murder, but your victim is still dead and her family misses her every day. You can be forgiven for sex before marriage, but you still may have the venereal disease. You can be forgiven for gossip, but people remain hurt. No matter how many times you say "I'm sorry," you can't fix past sins. It's best to not sin in the first place.

When you have sinned, make amends and commit yourself to doing right. Take your sin to God. Ask his forgiveness and his help to change your lifestyle (1 John 1:9). If you have hurt someone, ask his or her forgiveness. Do whatever you can to repair damage you've done. Then focus on living right today. Each time past sins tempt you, remember that God has forgiven you. Satan will try to get you down, so you can't concentrate on doing well today. Don't let the past ruin your future.

You can't lose God's love by doing wrong, but you can lose a lot of happiness. Don't let that happen.

■

What Is Guilt?

What if I don't feel guilty when I do or think something? Is it still wrong? What if I feel guilty when I'm doing right? Am I really doing wrong?

Guilt is a funny thing. Because it's a feeling it can get twisted by experiences or by Satan. Thus we need to inform feelings with the facts. Give guilt the attention it deserves, but don't let it be the sole determiner of your actions. Feelings are a good gift from God, but they aren't always accurate.

Wrong depends on reality, not our feelings about it. Reality is not what you define, what the law defines, or what the majority defines. Reality is the way things really are. If you have sex before you marry, you may get pregnant. That's reality. If you drink and drive, you may cause an accident that results in lifelong torment. That's reality. If you treat people with genuine concern, they will trust you. That's reality. If you confess your wrongs and try to do right, you will find joy. That's reality. If you focus on making another feel at home, you'll feel less lonely. That's reality. You can learn what's real and what's not by studying the Bible, by watching people, by listening to God. God cares enough to let you in on secrets only he can know.

Your experiences have much to do with how guilty you feel or don't feel. If you never got punished for anything and your parents always covered for you, you see no reason to behave. You don't feel bad for doing wrong. You see no connection between what you do and what happens. You won't feel guilty very often. Conversely, if your parents continually told you that you were no good and could do nothing right, you will feel guilty for almost everything you try and will feel every wrong is your fault. Ideally your parents rewarded you for good, punished you for bad, and loved you no matter what. You will then have a balanced sense of right and wrong.

If a serial killer feels no guilt, are his murders right? Of course not. Wrong is wrong no matter how people feel about it, and right is always right. It may be hard to believe, but it's always so. Discover what's right and wrong by studying the Bible. Then heed what you discover.

■

Temptation

I realize that my bad choices lead to bad effects but I don't always want to believe it. I feel so lonely when I refuse to do wrong that I want to give in. Just today the people at my table were talking about the girls at the next table. They called them names and ranked their bodies. I know it's not right to talk about girls like that, but it seems I'm the only one that sits out. Am I bad for being tempted? Would it really hurt to talk dirty once in a while? I can get forgiven.

Certainly God will forgive you. But God's forgiveness isn't meant to give you a margin of sin. God's forgiveness is designed to reunite you with him, to allow you to live with yourself again, to start over. You aren't bad when you're tempted, because temptation is not a sin. Giving in is.

God's rules aren't meant to take away your fun but to give you joy and to protect you from harm. If you talk about the girls the ways the guys at your lunch table do, you'll harm at least one person. That person might be one of the girls who hears your comment. It might be the very one you've been trying to get to like you. The one you hurt might be the guy at your table who's admired the way you care about girls rather than use them. He's been trying to get up his courage to stop. Your joining in the dirty talk takes away his chance. The one you hurt might be yourself—you'll see some girls as sex objects and some as rejects. Consequently, you'll treat them that way and will miss some of the greatest pleasures of relating to girls. You reap what you sow. Dirty talk harvests distance, loneliness, and alienation.

Think about the kind of relationship you want with a girl. Notice how God's rules make that more likely. God deepens love when he urges you to "not let any unwholesome talk come out of your mouths, but only what is helpful for building others up" (Ephesians 4:29). He knows when you sow genuine concern you'll reap closeness, harmony, and ever-increasing love.

Your struggle against temptation becomes easier when you recognize the delusion behind sin. As many teens agree, "The preacher says a true Christian won't find sin fun—but I do!" What do you find appealing about the lunch-table talk? What do you find appealing about other sins? The devil wouldn't have success if sin didn't look fun. The answer lies in deception. The devil makes wrong look right and right look boring. Talking about girls' bodies seems harmless and fun. But if you pursue the wrong, you will begin to see girls as objects rather than people. You hurt feelings. You miss other beauties in the girls.

Take a look at the following examples. What is the delusion behind each of these statements?

- "It was great—I got so drunk I couldn't remember anything I did or said."

- "Taking a candy bar or cassette tape from a store won't hurt. They build that into their prices."

- "We have birth control and we love each other so it's okay to have sex."

Learn to see things from Jesus' point of view—the human who lived most fully and loved most completely. Replace deception with reality. Notice the genuine acceptance you find by living according to God's guidelines.

■

Who Will Make My Life Complete?

Why doesn't anyone understand me? I yearn for someone who understands my deepest thoughts, encourages what I do, and applauds what I dream. Where and when will I find this one person who will make my life complete?

Seek no further. He's right beside you. Ultimately the only person who fully understands and is always there when you need him is God himself. The beauty of this arrangement is that God never leaves you, always has perfect advice, and understands both your past and your future. The frustration is that you want someone with skin on. The loveliest part is that God knows this. He made your yearnings for people. He knows best how to fulfill them and he will do so.

Caryn discovered this when her grandfather died. He had been the only one who really understood Caryn's struggles with overcoming shyness and with making new friends. He had given her courage to speak up and say hello. He had guided her step by step to like herself and feel confident. After his death Caryn felt no one would ever understand. But God gave Bill to Caryn. Bill understood, listened, encouraged, and brought out the best in her. Bill never replaced Caryn's grandfather but through Bill, God met the needs her grandfather had met. God knows your needs and will meet them with people. And don't forget: God will also use you to meet other people's needs. Notice how.

When you feel like no one really understands, no one really cares, no one really wants to be with you, turn to the One who always cares and the only One who can fully understand: God himself. Let him love you and guide you to find people who genuinely care, who want to be with you, and who bring out the best in you. Let him give you the skills you need to build lasting friendships, to communicate with and grow close to your parents, and to build mutual respect with teachers and other adults. Let him teach you how to become lovable, communicative, and caring. God is the source of your security, at-homeness, and happiness. He is the solution to your loneliness.

The point: God's care for you is the one unchanging constant in your life. Communicate with him continually, depend on his power, experience the security he gives, and discover the joy that comes through obeying him. Use your God-given freedom to truly love people, truly love God, and truly choose happiness.

■

Think It Through

1. How do you feel about God's total knowledge and total care of you? How does the way you feel about God impact how you respond to God?

2. When have you felt distant from God? What inaccurate conclusion brought about this distance? What fact helped you return to closeness?

3. What doubt or question have you asked about God or would you like to ask? How has (would) the answer drawn you close to God? To other people?

4. What makes your life a mess? What human choice(s) or circumstance brought this about? Most of the sad things that happen to us are the result of human choice, not God's design. Recall a time you blamed God for something God didn't do. What would God advise for handling this problem?

5. Why do bad things happen to good people? Good things to bad people?

6. What is the worst sin a person could commit? How does God's love transcend even this? Why should we be good if we can get forgiveness?

7. List something that does not tempt you and something that does. How might the way you resist nontempting things help you with tempting ones?

8. Why is God the only one who can ultimately solve your loneliness?

■

STUDY WITH A GROUP

Besides the questions and activities in
this section, don't forget to use the
"Think It Through" questions at the end of
each chapter to develop your lesson plans.

I'm the Only One Home on Weekend Nights

1. Give teenagers a lump of clay, and ask each teen to shape the clay into a shape that means "aloneness" to them. As each person explains his or her sculpture, notice that alone is a comfortable feeling for some and a lonely feeling for others. What's the difference between alone and lonely? How can alone time become comfortable?

2. Draw an intersecting arrow diagram (see page 15). Explain each arrow. Tilt the vertical arrow to a side and ask: What happens to friendships when our relationship with God gets out of alignment? What happens to our relationship with God when we have trouble with friends? What happens to friendships when we get back on track with God? (Straighten the arrow.) How can friends help us keep a direct relationship with God? Read Matthew 6:33.

3. Invite teens to name times they want to be alone and how alone time helps them.

4. Beginning with the person on your right, ask each teen to name something interesting to do while alone. Explain that no one can name what another person has said, and anyone who can't think of something waits until the next round. Keep a list and duplicate for the group to use during alone times.

5. Have teens spread out as far from each other as space allows. Provide paper and pencils, and guide them to write a letter to themselves that evaluates their care of others. Explain that lonely nights can mean you haven't been as loving to family and friends as you should have been. Suggest that they compliment each other for the loving things they do, and then recommend ways to each other that they might show their love. Call on volunteers to read

all or parts of their letters. Suggest that as we focus on others, there will be much less loneliness.

6. Give teens blank paper and guide them to write anonymous letters about the last time they were alone and lonely. Gather the letters and redistribute. Have each teen read the problem, diagnose, and recommend a cure. Discuss: What would God recommend? What actions or attitudes are needed? What is the worst way to deal with this problem? The best?

■

2

Even When I Go Places, I Still Feel Lonely

1. Invite the group to tell of times they felt lonely in a crowd. Why is crowd loneliness so miserable? What makes it happen? How do we fix it?

2. Have teens draw their idea of "the ultimate reject." Then ask: How is this person like you? What is likable about this person? Explain: We all feel like rejects sometimes, but deliberately welcoming all people can cut down on this feeling and build crowd closeness. Ask: How does seeing the good in people lessen loneliness in a crowd? Point out: Looking beyond certain actions and outer images helps us see the attractiveness in people.

3. Invite teens to dramatize conversations that make them feel lonely (like locker-room conversation). Ask: How can you feel comfortable doing right when right sounds boring or crazy? Encourage specific actions and words.

4. Divide the group into teams of four. Challenge each team to come up with twenty-six questions or discussion starters to be used at a party, composing one for each letter of the alphabet. For example, "Any homework this weekend?" "Been anywhere interesting lately?" Duplicate the list after class for teens to use.

5. Invite the group to name conversations they have messed up and ways they wish they had handled them differently. Invite them to practice for next time.

6. Have the group call out as many cut-downs or sarcastic comments as they can. Write the comments on a large piece of paper. Then choose one and have the group translate it to a positive way of saying the same thing. For example, "You airhead!" translates to "I like your relaxed style." "You'll never get it!" translates to "I

know you can do it—keep trying." Discuss: Why do we use sarcasm and cut-downs so frequently? How do they hurt? When is teasing appropriate? How can we compliment more?

■

3

When I Finally Make a Friend, We End Up Fighting

1. Post the saying: "True friends don't fight." Divide the group into two teams and have them debate the truth or falsehood of this statement. Emphasize that the best friends are those who solve problems, not those who have none.

2. Divide the group into two teams and have them list causes of friendship fights. To add interest, have each cause begin with the last letter of the former cause. For example: jealousy—you hurt me so I'll hurt you—understanding (lack of)—feelings of insecurity—you hurt someone I like—ego to protect—temper—real or imagined threat—think one is about to leave the other. See which team can come up with the longest list.

Use the lists to discuss questions like: How does knowing the cause of the fight help you know how to solve it? Name a cause and how to take care of it without a fight. Which causes impact you most strongly? How can God take care of each cause so we don't hurt our friends with it?

3. Display a room-length piece of yarn. Label one end "intentional" and one end "accidental." Direct teens to stand along the yarn at the place they think most friendship problems occur. Ask: How does this affect how you solve problems? Why?

4. Give each teen a slip of paper and have them jot down a problem they have had with a friend. Place the slips of paper in a bag and have pairs of teens choose one. Guide the pairs to role-play a discussion between two friends that would solve these problems. Encourage realism and honesty. Consider acting it out twice: once the way it usually happens, and once the way that will solve the problem rather than intensify it.

5. Go around the room asking each teen to name a practical joke that is fun and shows love.

---

6. Dramatize Jenny's using a friend to get what she wants. Ask: Why do we use friends? What's the difference between loyalty and using? What would you recommend in this situation and why?

7. Write in huge letters the word *anger*. Ask: How does anger start fights? How does anger make fights difficult to solve? How do fights keep us from staying friends? Have teens name an action, beginning with each letter in *anger*, that could solve anger. Guide teens to read Ephesians 4:25–29 for ideas.

8. Give teams of teens inexpensive clear umbrellas and markers that write on plastic. Challenge them to name actions and attitudes that keep people from being fair-weather friends. Ask: Which is the hardest to do? The easiest?

9. Ask the group to name circumstances that point to the end of a friendship.

10. Distribute stationery and instruct teens to write a letter to a friend that clears up a problem, asks forgiveness, or adds freshness to the friendship.

11. Close by sharing ways friends have helped with loneliness.

■

4

The Cliques Are Horrible at School and Church

1. Divide into teams of about four. Assign each a reason for cliques. Challenge teens to debate why their reason is the strongest. Then ask: What is the cure for each?

2. Give teens paper and colored pencils or crayons and have them draw someone who "fits in." Discuss: How can you tell if someone fits? Why do we want to be like him/her? Are there other ways to fit? How?

3. Provide paper and tape. Guide teams to write on each paper one action or discussion starter that could make new friends at school. Challenge teams to make the longest chain with the pages taped end to end.

4. Give teens a large piece of paper cut in the shape of glasses and direct them to write a prescription for clique blindness—how to see no cliques and how to cross clique lines.

5. Give each teen three index cards. Guide them to write on each a characteristic that makes a good group. Gather the cards and use these ways:

- Choose one and make a thirty-second speech on why it is important.

- Deal the cards. Each teen names the most valuable card in hand.

- Deal. Teens rank the cards in their hand from simplest to hardest. As each reports invite him or her to tell a specific way to do at least one action.

6. Call for each teen to name a command of God that brings happiness (for example: "Do not covet" keeps you happy with what you have). See Exodus 20 and Colossians 3 for commands. Invite teens to share ways they have encouraged each other to live for Christ at school.

7. Give teens paper plates and pencils. On the outside guide them to draw how they look at church. On the inside of the plate guide them to draw how they feel at church. After teens show both sides of their plates discuss with: What makes you feel accepted at church? Rejected? How do you help people feel accepted? Rejected? What cliques do we have (characteristics of cliques, not names of people) in our church? How can we become clique-free? What specific advice would Jesus Christ give us?

8. Spend time praying for the opening of cliques at school and church.

■

5

When Will I Be Loved?

1. Ask: What's the best way to get to know someone of the opposite sex? Why is sincerity important? Read David and Del's story. Give teens practice in genuineness by inviting each to tell something he or she likes to do. After each person shares, call for the group to tell why they like that activity. Review three steps to romantic happiness: (1) put God first, (2) believe you are lovable, (3) treat people well.

2. Make a list that gives suggestions for letting the opposite sex know you care. When the list is complete, have teens vote on the methods by holding up their fingers from 1—10, with 1 being "loser" and 10 being "works great." Invite other ideas and discussion. Use differences to point out there is no one right way to show interest.

3. Guide teens to write descriptions of the perfect sweetheart. Discuss with: Why do we look to boyfriends/girlfriends as the solution to loneliness? When have you been lonely even when dating? What does this say about the ability of romance alone to ease loneliness? Comment from the chapter introduction.

4. Guide half to argue why friendship should come before romance and half to argue why romance should come before friendship. Discuss: How do love and friendship enhance each other? Complicate each other? Differ?

5. Invite teens to draw or describe intimacy. (Don't limit it to physical intimacy.) Combine them into a single definition. Discuss: Why do we crave intimacy? How can we build it? What makes it scary? Inviting? Invite each teen to name one action or attitude that makes intimacy more probable.

---

6. To make dating more likely and better quality, guide guys and girls to give advice to one another. Direct them to write handbooks for the opposite sex including: What love is; how to let someone know you like them; how to get a date; what guys like in girls and what girls like in guys; dating pet peeves; what we search for in a woman/man; our dating thoughts and worries; why we date.

7. Guide teens to create a survival kit for breaking up. Suggest they use items from a first aid kit or tool box as object lessons. A tool box might include "tape keeps mouth from gossiping or getting revenge" and a "timer to give yourself healing time before jumping into a new relationship."

8. Pray by name for each teen's present and future romances.

■

6

My Dates and Friends Are Using Me

1. Provide a large sheet of paper and direct teams to draw users. Teens may choose to use symbols, words, or body outlines. Call for teams to display and describe the users. Ask: Why does your person use? How does he or she get away with it? How might you get your user to stop using?

2. Have teens read Matthew 5:38–42 and 7:6. Ask: How have you stopped using? Guide teens to develop a checklist that helps tell the difference between service and being used.

3. Guide teens to work in teams to compose a song that tells how sex, love, and using are related. Suggest formats like commercials, ballads, or raps. Discuss with: How is sex like love? Different? Why and how do people use with sex? How would you convince someone God's plan for sex is smartest?

4. Guide teens to draw a map with directions for finding a quality guy (for girls) or girl (for guys). Discuss with: Why do we play games in finding and growing love? How do we use? How would God help? Security? Confidence?

5. Invite teens to tell about an adult couple in love. How do you think they keep from using each other? How might you build a relationship like theirs?

6. Distribute bandages and ball point pens and invite teens to write on them an action, thought, or truth that can heal you after being used.

7. Read the friend descriptions in the last question and ask: How are these people good friends? Users? How might they be even better friends?

8. Distribute credit card sized papers. Challenge teens to write a vow such as: "I will treat people as irreplaceable, incredible, and invaluable." Ask: How does this give credit to people? To you?

9. Close with a time of prayer for courage and security to be genuine rather than scared, to cherish rather than use, to see each person as valuable.

■

7

My Parents Just Don't Understand

1. Explain the difference between authoritarian and authority. Ask: Why and when is authority needed in a family? Invite each teen to share at least one example. Ask: How can we get our parents to let us help in decision making?

2. Guide teens to draw or describe what would happen if there were no rules. Discuss with: Why do we need rules? If your parents had only one rule, what should it be? What danger do your parents' rules protect you from? What good do they encourage? What rules do you wish you had? What rule would you omit (or change) and why?

   Consider making a list of rules that the group agrees on. Offer the list to parents. Topics might include: curfew; consequences; treating people well; homework; free time; asking questions without being nosey; chores; trust.

3. Invite teens to share what they do while spending time with parents. Ask: How did you get started doing this? What else might you like to do? Encourage them to spend fun times with their parents.

4. Develop fool-proof plans for parents to find out what they need to know without teens feeling invaded. Ask: How can questioning build trust?

5. Lead role plays in which teens are the parents. Act out the way things are. Then act the way teens want things to be. Sample topics: lecturing, money, not showing care. Ask: How might we move from what is to what we need?

6. What action(s) has helped you and your parent(s) feel like you

are on the same team? Invite teens to share how they've overcome a problem with their parents.

7. Agree on a realistic amount of money and challenge teens to raise a family of four on it. Provide newspapers that give current prices for groceries, clothes, utilities, rent and more. Insist that prices be documented from the newspaper. Ask: What did you discover that would help your family?

8. Guide teens to write a loving letter to their parents telling why they love them, what they need from them, and in what ways they want to be close. Let teens deliver the letters.

■

My Teachers Never Like My Work

1. Invite teens to take turns calling out their greatest frustration with a teacher. Topics include homework, getting on a bad side, not being able to concentrate, rules, not caring anymore. After each frustration is named, invite the group to call out advice. For "too much homework," others might name "study when you first get home"; "grin and bear it"; "ask for mercy."

2. Divide teens into "going into junior high" and "going into senior high." Provide a panel of teens for each group to answer questions about how to survive in junior high/senior high. Use sensitive teens for the panels. To get things going, have each panel member share three tips.

3. Go around the circle and direct each teen to name a way to be smart. Each must name something different. Guide each teen to privately choose at least one way they are smart. Pause to thank God for making everyone smart.

■

I Don't Even Like Myself

1. Guide pairs of teens to write formulas for healing after failure.

2. Write on cards these and other potential reasons people have trouble liking themselves: Our world emphasizes outer beauty; fairy tales about beautiful princes and princesses; put-downs; rejection; commercials emphasize beauty; family isn't as strong; we're not busy enough so have time to worry; we're too busy; Satan; don't believe God made us; parent or significant other rejects us. Guide each teen to choose a card from your hand and speak for thirty seconds on why the reason is true. Then invite the group to argue good-naturedly about which reason is strongest.

3. To help teens become comfortable with their physical appearance, have them write a letter to their bodies. Post these sentence starters to prompt ideas: "Dear Body: I'm glad God gave you to me because ..."; "I wish you were more _____ but I'm very glad you _____"; "One thing I've learned to appreciate about you is ..."; "An inner quality I want to show through you is ..." Invite volunteers to read their letters but force no one.

4. Offer an opportunity for teens to share a private thought or question that they've held inside but now want to talk about. Encourage sensitivity.

5. Guide teens to repeat for each member: "You _____ (name) are a person of worth created by God. We care about you."

I Wonder If Even God Has Rejected Me

1. Distribute paper and display colored pencils or markers. Direct teens to draw God. Supplement with the six evidences for God in the second question. Ask: When do you doubt God's presence? His existence? How do you know God is real even in the midst of your doubts? How do you know he cares personally? How do these facts impact your daily choices?

2. Assure teens that it is not bad to question God. Ask: Why are questions good (give understanding, remove fear, etc.) ? Guide teens to write questions they have about God. Read these and moderate as teens answer them for each other. Encourage answers based on the Bible.

3. Guide teens to take turns telling about the worst day in their lives. Jot down the evil, painful, and sad events they mention. Call out events from the speeches. Ask: What caused this? When and why do we blame God for things he had nothing to do with? How can God help someone through this?

4. Guide teens to write down what they think the unpardonable sin is. Clarify with Matthew 12:32 and Luke 12:10. Stress that the only unpardonable sin is rejecting God.

5. Post signs that say AGREE, DISAGREE, STRONGLY AGREE, STRONGLY DISAGREE on the four walls of your room. Read statements based on questions in this chapter and direct teens to stand under the sign that tells how they feel about these statements. Call on at least one teen in each group to tell why they chose as they did. Notice the many facets of truth they bring out. Sample statements: (1) We can know without a doubt God is real; (2) We can prove God exists even though we can't see or touch him; (3) Doubts draw me closer to God; (4) Most bad things

happen because of people's poor choices; (5) Bad events in my life mean God is mad at me; (6) If you don't feel guilty, it's okay to do it; (7) God doesn't mind if you sin a little; (8) It is possible to avoid temptation; (9) We don't need human understanding because God understands; (10) God is the solution to loneliness problems.

6. Guide teens to list sins that tempt them or don't seem wrong. Direct teens to take turns taking one and telling the pain that sin will cause. Direct them to list opposite actions and why they bring joy.

7. Invite teens to tell times they felt close to God and far from him. Determine what makes the difference and how to grow closeness again.

8. Ask: If you could give only one sentence of advice on overcoming loneliness, what would it be?

■